MY LAND IS DYING

by Harry M. Caudill
Night Comes to the Cumberlands
Dark Hills to Westward
My Land Is Dying

HARRY M. CAUDILL
MY LAND IS DYING

E. P. DUTTON & CO., INC. | NEW YORK | 1971

Published simultaneously in Canada
by Clarke, Irwin & Company Limited, Toronto and Vancouver

Library of Congress Catalog Card Number: 76-158582
SBN 0-525-16230-5

Grateful acknowledgment is given to *Dun's* magazine for permission to reprint portions of "America's Most Profitable Company?" by Thomas Murphy, from *Dun's,* April, 1965, Copyright, 1965, Dun & Bradstreet Publications Corporation.

PICTURE CREDITS
Bob Gomel: pages 36-37, 39, 40, 41, 44, 45, 46-47, 49, 55, 98.   Jean Martin: pages 38, 42, 48, 54, 100. John Fetterman: pages 43 (top), 50-51, 93 (top). *The New York Times:* pages 52, 91, 92, 94-95.   Billy Davis, *The Courier-Journal:* page 43 (bottom). American Metal Climax, Inc.: pages 96, 97.   U.S. Geological Survey: page 99.   Milton Rogovin: pages 4, 8.

I should like to express my gratitude
to the Field Foundation for its support

That they may know some cared,
this book is dedicated
to all those unborn millions
who must someday
inhabit America's spoil banks

Early in the 1960s Harry Caudill's strong voice became known to many people outside of his native region. In magazine articles and most especially in *Night Comes to the Cumberlands* (1963), Mr. Caudill revealed himself to be an eloquent and forceful spokesman for the mountain people of Appalachia. He is a lawyer who lives in Whitesburg, where the courthouse that dominates Letcher County, Kentucky, stands—just another building to the outsider, but oh the power that is concentrated there. For Mr. Caudill it has been urgently necessary that such power, exercised by a few men for their own benefit and the benefit of giant corporations located in distant cities like Pittsburgh and New York and Boston, be exposed and revealed as one of the causes of misery and extreme poverty among thousands of American families up the creeks and hollows of West Virginia and western North Carolina and eastern Tennessee as well as his home state. Nor was he, nearly a decade ago, quite without important sources of potential interest if not outright support. John F. Kennedy had come to know those "folks" way up the hills in the course of his quest for the presidency, and for all the talk (by various "observers" and social scientists) of their self-centeredness and parochialism and suspiciousness, not to mention the streak of anti-Catholicism in them (among other Americans), the people of West Virginia had been noticeably impressed by the earnest young man from Massachusetts, who seemed determined to take an interest in the nation's poor and vulnerable citizens, be they in our cities or rural Southerners or mountaineers or on government reservations or (as migrant farmers) just about everywhere.

No matter that he spoke with a broad Boston accent, and was rich, and had gone to Harvard; he was an active, energetic man and he addressed himself directly to the needs of people unaccustomed to being sought out by anyone for anything. So, they voted for him, and when he was President began to feel some hope. Meanwhile Harry Caudill was speaking up for them and their cause, and for a while it seemed that the whole nation was listening. A "War on Poverty" was declared. Youthful activists bent on social and political action began to appear in those isolated hills and valleys. Communities were encouraged to "organize," set down their "goals" or "priorities." Television crews arrived, anxious to capture on films the sorrow and pain and suffering of a proud and sensitive people, in need of work and money, but by no means anxious to be held up to the nation as merely pitiable. Then, all of a sudden it was all over. By the end of the 1960s Appalachia's poor were again largely forgotten. John Kennedy and his brother Robert were dead. A disastrous war in Asia was tearing the nation apart, not to mention bleeding it badly of its men, wealth, and resources. As a consequence recession and inflation alike threatened "the economy," another way of describing the lives of millions of human beings. And Harry Caudill's Appalachia—again it would simply have to sit back and be patient and take it on the chin and trust in some better day that no one could really foresee.

I recite that recent history because in a way it helps us measure the courage and tenacity and integrity of this book's author. He did not have to persist in his ways, keep pointing out to anyone who would pay attention how meanly and dishonestly and cruelly and mischievously the mountaineers of states like Kentucky and West Virginia have been treated over the years. Other "options," as it is put these days, were open to him. He had said his piece; he could have softened its tone, undercut its message enough to please all sorts of powers and principalities—in which case grateful county officials and corporation lawyers and regional "representatives" of the federal bureaucracy would have acknowledged him as a seer of sorts, a wise and venerable man, a man who understands what is "practical," a man who wants to be "constructive" and not cause "harm" to the "system." Perhaps he would now be a federal judge, or a high official in his state government. Perhaps he would be on one of those local or national commissions—always the reward a "safe" man gets when nervous politicians cast about for allies in the face of one or another "problem."

Instead Mr. Caudill has persisted; he has again and again reminded this nation how much remains to be done: up there in those hollows are families near penniless, and for that to be the case in the world's richest, mightiest nation is a scandal. But beyond the tragedies Appalachia's people must live with every day—the hunger and malnutrition and high infant mortality rate and widespread joblessness—there is yet another tragedy still being enacted there. Thousands and thousands of acres of land have been, are right now being, or are soon scheduled to be cut into—*stripped* is the all too emphatic and suggestive and appropriate word—so that coal can be obtained and shipped to America's ever needy industrial empire. Never mind that beautiful trees are felled. Never mind that flowers and shrubs and meadows are covered over. Never mind that clear streams and creeks and rivers become slow-moving monsters: acid kills fish; poisonous mud is deposited all over and kills grass, not to mention the wild life that ordinarily sticks close to water. Never mind that farms are destroyed, and homes, and roads, and indeed entire hills, entire settlements of people. Coal is needed by factories and power companies and the TVA, so coal will be obtained—quickly and efficiently and directly. As for those who worry about land being destroyed, water polluted, wildlife killed—they are willful troublemakers, or cranky social critics, or at best they are romantics, hopelessly unable to appreciate the contemporary needs of an "advanced" nation like ours.

There can be no doubt that Mr. Caudill is a troublemaker: he objects to the exploitation of man and his environment by companies that behave as if they are a law unto themselves. Caudill is also a social critic, and he is indeed cranky, because he cannot stomach what he sees happening every day: the poor being made yet poorer, the rich getting more and more, all under the protection of federal laws and state laws and, ultimately, the guns that sheriffs and their deputies use up those Appalachian hills. And he is a "romantic," too; yes, if a "romantic" is one who has an old-fashioned sense of justice and fair play, and if he is one who treasures the Declaration of Independence and the Constitution and believes they ought to be honored not with lip service but in deed, then beyond any question Harry Caudill is a "romantic."

In this book Mr. Caudill expands his already large vision: he concentrates his keen mind on the problem of strip mining as a *national* issue. He warns us that Appalachia's misery is soon going to be appreciated by the rest of us—not because we will have gone there and tried to experience firsthand what the region's people have to contend with day after day, but rather because in the Southwest and in our central states and along our eastern seaboard there are those who want things like coal or oil, and go take them—regardless of the costs to people and their natural surroundings. Meanwhile the rest of us seem destined to stand by in silent dismay or helpless rage. So it goes we say—and hope for the best and often enough expect the worst.

For Harry Caudill there is an alternative, though. As a writer he wants to bring an outrageous and continuing crime to the public's attention. But as an experienced lawyer and social activist he wants us all to do something: bring our energies together, make known our sentiments—in order to counter the maneuvers of all those corporate officials and corporation lawyers and sub-servient bureaucrats, not to mention the all too compliant judges and sheriffs who do what they're told to do, namely the bidding of "the big boys, the rich boys," as one mountaineer I know has a way of putting it. (If only some of our sociologists and political scientists spoke half as bluntly.) I have no way of knowing whether Harry Caudill's struggle is of any avail; I am sure he himself must live with nightmares, must all the time find himself ready to wake up one morning and find the whole of Appalachia leveled—become a sort of vast wasteland of bubbling acid and sludge and dead trees and the litter of homes abandoned and often enough interred in mud. Nevertheless, he keeps on strug-gling. He writes, he fights in the courts, he speaks to people, he does all he can—and more than most of us. A more enlightened nation would honor him as one of its finest citizens; but then, a more enlightened nation would not be so in need of his kind of extraordinary public service.

—*Robert Coles*

July, 1971
Harvard University

One day in the spring of 1965, I climbed a hill with Dan Gibson, a wrinkled, weather-beaten man of eighty. He had lived all his days in Knott County, Kentucky, near the geographic heart of the Appalachian range. He had seen, as the mountain people put it, many "times of trouble," and his eyes were deeply troubled now.

Near the top we came to a halt, and Dan leaned on a heavy stick. For a long while we looked in silence at the valley and across it to the ridges whose crests merged with the horizon. Above those timbered crests, John James Audubon had once recorded how he saw the sky darkened by vast crowds of passenger pigeons in flight. The hardwood forests that clothed the Appalachians in Audubon's day were the largest of their kind and among the oldest and grandest in the world. Dan Gibson himself had witnessed the cutting of their gigantic walnut, oak, and tulip poplar trees to make way for cornfields and pastureland, and later he had watched the prop-cutters sawing down the new growth to be used in the mines. Once again, after the onslaught of the coal industry, he had seen the gashed land struggle to heal itself with new growth. But the stillness that lay over it now seemed to portend, this time, a different fate.

On other hills in that part of Kentucky, nodding in deep coves and over rocky ledges, wild flowers were in bloom, snakes sunned themselves, and squirrels darted overhead. Though diminished from its former magnificence, the forest still pulsed with growth and activity, the marvelous fabric of interdependent life still intact. Here, the scene was altogether different: jumbled mounds of loose earth, slabs of bluish slate, half-buried trunks of dead trees, pools of stagnant, acid-yellowed water, and raw cliffs of sandstone newly scoured; a litter of mechanical relics, already rusting, from the bulldozers, trucks, and power shovels whose work, completed, had left this desolation behind.

Dan Gibson was a coffinmaker by trade. Years ago, an accident had severed two or three fingers from his right hand. Death and injury were no strangers to him. But they had not inured him to sorrow. "The strip miners are killing these old hills," he said at last. "When they finish, there won't be anything left. My ancestors lived here, and I've got a stepson in Vietnam who wants to come back here and live out his days too." He paused. "Yes, sir, this is my land"—the maimed hand gestured toward the landscape —"and my land is dying."

As we walked back to Dan Gibson's house, and I reflected on the millions of acres in America that have likewise been maimed by industry, his words rang in my ears like those of a latter-day Jeremiah.

MY LAND IS DYING

The mountainous eastern half of Kentucky is about the same size as Switzerland. A fifth of Switzerland is rocky and barren or sheathed perpetually in ice and snow. Its forests are limited in extent and variety. Beds of salt are its only important mineral resource. But there are six million Swiss people. Swiss banks are a power throughout the world. Swiss factories are so numerous and productive that workers must be imported—and these workers alone outnumber the entire population of eastern Kentucky. Illiteracy in Switzerland has been reduced almost to zero. Its standard of living is one of the highest in the world.

If there had been a decent regard for the land in eastern Kentucky, its mountaineers might have thrived like the Swiss. Not only are the Appalachian forests unmatched as a supply of hardwood timber, but underground there are valuable deposits of coal, petroleum, natural gas, limestone, low-grade iron ore, silica, and brines rich in chemicals. Every acre of its soil is arable. But a misguided policy of extraction has brought grief and poverty to its inhabitants. For generations they have mined and quarried and sawed and shipped away the riches of the region. The people who live along its winding creeks—Carr's Fork, Troublesome, Grapevine, Beaver, Quicksand, Rockhouse, and Kingdom Come—are nearly all descendants of the pioneer settlers who gave the streams their names. Now they number only three-quarters of a million, nearly a third of whom are on public assistance. More and more of those who can are moving elsewhere, while those who remain sink deeper into apathy.

I was born in the Cumberland region of Kentucky; its expiring loveliness is a part of me. But the same forces that are bringing ruin to Appalachia are now a threat wherever technological competence is yoked with human avarice and folly. Wherever the profit motive is still exalted as a virtue, the urge to acquire and to consume becomes a frenzy. In our own nation, industry, the banks, the farm organizations and labor unions, the churches and foundations, and every aspect of government continually whip up and urge on this almost mindless drive. Our institutions stand guard over the status quo in a time when only sweeping changes in attitude and practice can save us from our own human folly. This generation may be the last one granted the opportunity to act before it is too late.

In Kentucky, twelve thousand acres a year are being strip-mined, and each year the operation is accelerated. This means that each year an expanse covering nearly twenty-four square miles is denuded of vegetation, the surface is piled high with cap rock, and streams that once ran clear are transformed into acid-yellowed rivulets of mud. And each year the human exodus continues. The mountaineers, finding it no longer possible to live at all in a landscape given over to coal augers, dynamite, trucks, and bulldozers, and to laws that protect the operators from the poor but not the poor from the operators, are disappearing into urban ghettos. According to the 1970 census, 80,727 Kentuckians had left the state since 1960—mainly from the coal counties, where a single industry has perfected the art of being a bad neighbor to all living things, including man. And unless the trend is reversed, a rapidly developing earthmoving technology will eventually bring the same methods to nearly every one of the fifty states.

Elsewhere in the world, meanwhile, coal production is being curtailed or entirely halted as a matter of social policy. In Belgium—the world's most highly industrialized nation—coal operations are being ended because of their heavy social and environmental costs, and because the miners are needed by other industries. Such industrial countries are turning increasingly to the United States as a supplier of coal. Japan alone purchased more than twenty million tons of coal in 1969. At present rates of growth, purchases of coal by Japan will exceed forty million tons annually by 1973. The total exports of coal in 1970 came to eighty million tons. This demand is having an impact on prices. In the first seven months of 1970, many coal shippers not bound by long-term contracts were able to raise their prices by 100 percent. After a slump, the market for coal has been rejuvenated. And the story of that rejuvenation is largely summed up in the roar of an entire new generation of machines that amount to a redefinition of the word "mining." Tunneling underground may give way entirely to the methods these machines make possible.

For example, near Cumberland, Ohio, the Central Ohio Coal Company now boasts one known as "Big Muskie," currently acclaimed as the world's largest earthmoving machine. Tourists pause daily on the highways to watch as it devours the Ohio landscape. Tall as a 32-story building, it consumes enough electricity to supply a small city. A boom 310 feet long is fitted with a bucket that lifts 325 tons of soil at a gulp, controlled by steel cables five inches in diameter. This behemoth weighs 27 million pounds, and the millions of dollars it cost can be justified only by keeping it busy night and day throughout the year.

In 1967, the U.S. Department of the Interior sent to the Congress a detailed study entitled *Surface Mining and Our Environment*. Its findings were based on data from many sources, including state and federal agencies and industry-sponsored studies. As of January 1, 1965, according to that report, a total of 3.2 million acres throughout the fifty states had been ravaged by strip mining. The disturbance had been smallest in Hawaii, with only ten acres, and greatest in Pennsylvania, with a total of 370,202 acres affected. In Kentucky, the total came to 127,700 acres—a figure exceeded by those for Ohio (276,700), West Virginia (195,500), Florida (188,800), California (174,020), Texas (163,300), Illinois (143,100), and Alabama (133,900). These figures represented the extraction of sand and gravel, stone, clay, phosphate rock, iron ore, and gold in addition to coal and lignite, which accounted for 40 percent of the total, embracing some 1,302,000 acres. Of these acres, 665,000, or more than half, were in the Appalachian region, where another 105,000 acres had been stripped for other minerals. By the beginning of 1970, the total stripped in the same region for coal and other minerals combined had risen to more than a million acres. In Georgia, for example, 2,000 acres have been stripped in the quest for kaolin, a clay used in the manufacture of porcelain. In North Carolina, the Gibbsite Corporation plans to mine no less than 25,000 acres for the hydrated aluminum oxide that gives the company its name—an operation its spokesmen piously assert will bring economic gains without environmental loss.

Elsewhere it is the same story. In Florida, the digging of phosphate rock is mainly responsible for the tens of thousands of acres of devastation. Even the fertile croplands of the Midwest are not exempt. What is happening in Iowa is instructive. Under its rich black soil—the most fertile on earth, extending in places to a depth of forty feet—lies coal, about twenty-four billion tons of it. Low grade though it is by Appalachian standards, it is there and even now it is being mined. By the end of 1964, eleven thousand acres had been stripped for coal, plus thirty-three thousand more for clay, stone, and other minerals. During the last six years, another three thousand acres have been mined for coal alone, and the industry is growing. Approximately 40 percent of the state can be strip-mined by the technological means now available; and unless substitutes for coal are speedily found, it almost certainly will be. Already, here as in Indiana and Illinois, mining companies are acquiring easements from farmers, some of whom are wealthy but who cannot resist the lure of further profit.

The same melancholy drama is being enacted in the Southwest. In 1964, "progressive" Indians of the Navajo nation persuaded their brethren that strip mining for coal on reservation lands would be a good thing. Despite all their previous disastrous experience with whites—cavalrymen, missionaries, and bureaucrats —somehow the elders of the tribe reached the conclusion that the Peabody Coal Company would be different. As a result, sixty-four thousand acres, containing an estimated two hundred million tons of bituminous coal, were leased for extraction by "strip, auger, underground or other generally approved mining methods." Economic pressure had driven the Navajos to sign the lease—just as it had led thousands of poor and ignorant Appalachian farmers to sign away their rights, seventy-five years ago, to the interests that are now systematically destroying the region.

No nation was ever more abundantly endowed with natural beauty than ours. Yet it is clear from this continuing record that no nation has been more heedless of its legacy. And no chapter of that record is uglier or more threatening than the chapter that continues to be written by the mining interests, whether below or on the surface of the land.

CHAPTER II

The coal-bearing region of eastern Kentucky embraces twelve entire counties and parts of as many more. Its hills, capped with picturesque crags of sandstone, rise near the state's southern border to an elevation of forty-four hundred feet. Along the north face of Pine Mountain, cliffs of blue white limestone tower for a hundred miles in an unbroken escarpment. The vegetation of the area is what ecologists call "mixed mesophytic forest," denoting a well-drained habitat and a climate midway between wet and dry. In this part of the Appalachian range, temperatures rarely exceed ninety degrees or fall as low as zero. The annual rainfall averages nearly fifty inches, more than in any other part of the continent except the Pacific Northwest. With more than a hundred different species, there is a greater variety of trees here than anywhere in the northern hemisphere, with the possible exception of eastern China.

Long before the geologic upheaval that produced the Appalachians, the region was part of a vast swampland forested with tree-sized club mosses and ferns. From the accumulated debris of these primitive plants, throughout hundreds of millions of years, the organic deposits settled and were compacted into coal—a mineral residue estimated at some thirty-five billion tons. As its weight increased, the earth's crust buckled under it, rearing the long ridge we know as the Appalachians far above the continental floor. During the two hundred million years that have elapsed since that cataclysmic event, later and gentler uplifts have perpetuated the mountainous character of the region, and the forests that clothe the Cumberlands and the Great Smokies have undergone the long evolution that accounts for their unique and unrivaled beauty.

It was early in the geologic era known as the Tertiary, beginning some seventy million years ago, that these eastern forests reached their maximum extent. While the Rockies were no more than low hills, and even mild temperatures prevailed in the Arctic zone, unbroken woodlands extended westward across the continent and northward to Alaska, where over land bridges long since submerged they continued their advance southward into eastern Asia. The record of their extent is preserved in fossil remains—the leafprints of sycamores in Colorado, of magnolias in Canada and along the shores of Greenland. In eastern China today, those same magnolias live on, along with spicewood, sweet gum, sassafras, and an understory of ferns and flowering plants common to the two regions but no longer found anywhere else in the world.

Following that advance came the upheavals, beginning some twenty or thirty million years ago, that produced the Rockies. This immense mountain chain, extending from Canada to New Mexico, acted as a barrier to the moisture-laden winds from the Pacific, and as their burden of rain and snow descended on its rugged western face, the central stretches of the continent became too dry to support trees. The region became a grassland, and the forest retreated eastward to where rain carried inland from the Atlantic would permit it to thrive.

Then the once-mild Arctic regions turned cold. Over millions of years, the northern hardwood forests were driven southward for thousands of miles, to be replaced by the firs and spruces that had once been restricted to frigid mountaintops. About a million years ago, as the cold deepened, came the era of the frozen Pleistocene, with its spreading glaciers. At their greatest extent, these great shields of slowly advancing ice covered all of New England and reached southward into Ohio and Pennsylvania. The movement of the glaciers was so slow that northern trees such as the spruces and firs managed to survive by inching southward, until they had invaded the peaks of the Smokies. They survive there today, glacial relics among the magnolias and pawpaws of the South.

As the ice slowly melted and the glaciers retreated, they left in their wake a vast bleak expanse across the northern half of the continent. Everywhere, in drifts, heaps, and sheets, lay immense loads of ground-up rock deposited by the glaciers. The layer of soil and humus that had been built up through eons of growth and decomposition had been bulldozed out of existence by the action of the moving ice. The same kind of devastation is now being accomplished, on a smaller scale but at much greater speeds, by the earthmoving machinery in use today.

South of the ice sheet at its greatest extent, climates were much colder than they are now, but not so cold as to destroy the vegetation of the region. In protected coves and valleys of the southern Appalachians, the hardwood forest survived, a vast storehouse of seeds that would eventually reclothe and reclaim the naked land. At the edge of the glacier, the first plants to reappear were of northern origin, able to thrive in the sparse soil and the damp, cold climate prevailing there—the spruce and fir, the bunchberry and bead lily. These hardy pioneers began the infinitely slow process, among the rubble and even on the bare rock, of rebuilding and replenishing the soil, preparing the way for plants that needed a richer environment to survive. As the climate slowly moderated, white pine, yellow birch, and sugar maple moved northward, replacing the stands of spruce and fir, to be followed in their turn by oak, beech, and tulip trees. Not all of the species that had lived on in the Appalachian coves were hardy enough to survive the extremes of alternating heat and cold, moisture and drought, that were tolerated by the botanical pioneers. Some, such as the white basswood and the yellow buckeye, needed the protection of rich humus and a long-established forest. Others could endure cold but not drought: these, including the beech, sugar maple, yellow birch, and hemlock, spread northward into New England and westward across Canada into Wisconsin. Still others, tolerant of both drought and cold, moved westward as well as northward, finally thinning out as they reached the central prairies. The chestnut oaks progressed only as far westward as Indiana; the hickories, and some other oaks, spread to form scattered stands as far west as Iowa. The tulip tree, a member of the magnolia family, which needs rich soil as well as moisture, made its way north through Indiana into southern Michigan, and westward to the borders of Illinois, where it survives today only in the most luxuriant habitat. But the forest that reclaimed the devastation left by the glaciers was far thinner and less varied than that of the Cumberland region, counting less than a fifth the number of species even at its finest. Undisturbed aeons would be required to produce the deep, rich soil of the Cumberland Plateau. Meanwhile, a new disturbing force has obtruded on the slow and majestic processes of nature. That force is human civilization and the process known, with unintended irony, as "development." Because of it, the question now becomes not whether the age-old forest may one day spread to new regions, but whether it can survive at all.

Forty-five centuries before the first white men entered the Cumberlands, the region was dotted with Indian villages. These aborigines held the land in veneration, and they moved through it as harmlessly as the mists that rise and settle among the hollows. In the broader valleys, they built their clustered huts and surrounded them with palisades of sharpened stakes. While the squaws pulled up the wild cane and planted their corn, the men hunted deer and bear on the hillsides and tracked bison to the canebrakes that flourished in the lowland. Instead of cutting trees for fuel, the squaws gathered fallen branches to keep cooking fires ablaze. When a campsite became polluted with human wastes, the inhabitants simply moved on and built a new village a few miles away.

The first white men to penetrate the Cumberland region were hunters who left home and family behind for months while they roved through the uncleared wilderness. Settlers did not begin arriving until after 1794, when the Battle of Fallen Timbers had broken the hold of the Indian tribes on the territory lying between the Appalachians to the east and the Ohio and Miami rivers to the west. The treaty of Greenville, signed August 3, 1795, between General Anthony Wayne and an assembly of tribal chiefs, confirmed the victory, and an Act of Congress on May 19, 1796, set the eastern boundaries of what was to be Indian territory— boundaries which the westward-moving frontiersmen proceeded to ignore.

Unlike the aboriginal inhabitants, these settlers never found a rapport with the land. In a sense, with the building of the first crude cabins the land began to die. Like the Indians before them, the settlers began by digging up the wild cane and planting corn in its place. Thenceforward, however, a settler when he was not hunting was clearing the ground for ever larger fields of corn and of beans and potatoes. But instead of frugally collecting dead branches for firewood, these pioneers systematically killed the trees by girdling the bark with an ax. They brought in cattle and razorback swine, turning them loose to browse and trample the cornfields after the crop had ripened, thus paving the way for devastating erosion. For thirty years, a steady stream of new immigrants poured into the wooded hills and valleys of the Cumberlands. The birthrate was high, and the wilderness was looked upon as an adversary to be conquered. The Indians had inhabited the region; the white man promptly began to use it up. Within two or three generations the pressures on the land began visibly to take their toll.

In the early years, hunting was a source of income. So many deer were taken that deerskin became the equivalent of cloth, and the hides were so widely used for barter that they took the place of money—a practice that has left behind the word "buck" as slang for "dollar." Around 1810, Napoleon Bonaparte sent a purchasing agent to the village of Louisa, on the Big Sandy River, in search of black bear pelts for use by the Grand Armée. In many districts, the mountaineers hunted the bears to extinction, seeking them out in the caves where they hibernated and killing them by the dozen before they could awaken from their winter sleep. The skins went to France, and most of them probably were lost somewhere in the snows of the Russian winter.

Inexorably, the game began to disappear. As their numbers multiplied, the settlers found that the land they had cleared could no longer support them and provide fodder for their horses and cattle. These wielders of ax and rifle knew nothing of cover-cropping to preserve the soil's fertility and prevent erosion. As generations passed, their isolation deepened. There were no roads and hardly any schools. Without industry, skills, or profitable crafts, they could only cling to their primitive agriculture. Trapped in a descending cycle of toil, poverty, and futility, they turned to clearing the hillside coves as their fathers had cleared the bottomlands. But their labor with ax and plow could not keep pace with their needs. By the middle of the Civil War, the people of the Cumberlands were starving. The final blow had come as bushwhackers and foragers for the contending armies plundered the corncribs and smokehouses of the mountaineers. Abraham Lincoln became the first President to order relief, in the form of food, for the poor of Appalachia.

After the war, a building boom sent timber purchasers into the Cumberlands, and great "log runs" carried millions of felled trees downriver to the sawmills. In some areas, narrow-gauge railroads were built, and the chugging locomotives mingled with the whine of saws and the crash of falling trees. The village of Louisa now expanded into the world's largest outlet for hardwood lumber—a distinction it was to hold for thirty years. In a prolonged orgy of felling and hauling, the finest trees were the first to be cut. Then came those of lower quality. Lumber from virgin groves of

Appalachia went into the building of houses and ships, into cooperage for whiskey and hogsheads for tobacco. No seed trees were left except by accident or, occasionally, because of inaccessibility. A region of immeasurable antiquity, where once for miles no tree had been felled, no stream had been sullied, no furrow cut—a region whose huge and ancient trees, whose caves, cliffs, and wind-carved arches had been regarded with veneration by the Indians—had been so altered that for us its primeval majesty is all but impossible to imagine.

Then, after 1900, came the railroads, and the coal industry came with them. Along the three major streams of the region—the Big Sandy, the Kentucky, and the Cumberland—coal towns sprang up as hundreds of tunnels were driven into the ground. Some of the deposits lay as deep as 150 feet or more. Others striated the hillsides in bands ranging from a few inches to as much as fourteen feet thick. As the tunneling proceeded, wooden props by the millions were in demand. To supply them, the beeches, poplars, oaks, pines, and hickories that the lumber cutters had missed now came down, big trees and young saplings together. And all the while, the clearing of new ground for cornfields continued almost unabated. Hundreds of thousands of acres of timber were reduced to bare earth, gullied to the bedrock, and shielded by no vegetation but the spare, wiry tufts of broom sedge.

The devastation left by the cutting opened the way to a new enemy—fire. The litter of chips, leaves, bark, and branches among the dying stumps could be set ablaze by lightning or a carelessly dropped match. A fire might smolder among leaves on the ground for days at a time, to be whipped by sudden dry winds into an inferno that soon roared through whatever neighboring timber remained. Neither the state nor any of the counties affected had provisions for dealing with forest fires, which sometimes raged unchecked for an entire season. Finally, during the 1920s, a fungus negligently imported from the Orient reached the Cumberlands, and within a few years all of the region's splendid chestnut stands had fallen victim to the blight.

These forces had so depleted the forests of the Cumberland region that before the end of World War II they appeared doomed to vanish within a few decades. Meanwhile, the cropland was visibly failing as well. Seven generations of scratch-farming along the hillsides and the ribbons of bottomland had made the task of living from the soil increasingly hard. By 1939 the average yield of corn per acre was down to sixteen bushels—barely enough to fatten a hog or two, supply the family table with mush and corn bread, and keep the plow mule alive through another winter. To eke out a marginal existence, thousands of Kentucky farmers worked in the mines as well, thus dealing with their own hands another blow to the land they had loved and misused for a century.

Then came the use of roof bolting with steel ties to replace the wooden mine props. In a further jolt to the economy, mechanization of the mines left thousands of men idle. There was a growing exodus of hill people to the industrial cities of Indiana, Ohio, Illinois, and Michigan, and with it a new stillness descended on the ravaged land. Young poplars sprang up in abandoned cornfields, and pines took root among the scarred expanse of broom sedge. Slowly the depleted wildlife began returning. The scars left by coal tipples began gradually to heal as the rows of empty mining shacks collapsed and were overgrown with vines. But those who saw hope in this reprieve had not reckoned with the greater threat to come.

To know the ancient mountain range that parallels our Atlantic Coast is to love it. The Appalachians are a labyrinth of hills, mountains, broad valleys, narrow hollows, swift creeks, and splendid rivers. Its wrinkled maze is indescribably old—predating the Rockies by scores of millions of years.

A spoil bank in eastern Kentucky three years after strip mining. Extractive industries in Appalachia have hauled away quantities of ores, fuels, and wood—about $500 billion worth in the last 130 years.

These scenes are not limited to the Appalachians. Strip miners are working some 1.2 million acres in twelve Eastern states; the coal rush of the 1970's will carve up twice that acreage west of the Mississippi. Even the Navajo Indian lands in the Southwest are now being stripped by the Peabody Coal Company.

To reach the coal seams, a bulldozer strips the earth from the seam,
following the black ore around the contour of a mountain. This leaves a
gash, similar to a cut made for a road. Power shovels scoop
up the coal that lies exposed.

Augers—huge rotating bits up to seven feet in diameter
—bore into the mountain to bring out the remainder of the seam.

Sulfur, associated with coal-bearing formations,
enters streams, and a solution of sulfuric acid results.

New deserts are being created throughout America:
Permits to strip federal land doubled in 1970;
states to be heavily mined include Arizona,
Colorado, Montana, and Wyoming.

The sham of an industry "reclamation program"
—the spray contains grass seed.

Overleaf: Long ago the settlers in Appalachia sold their right to the minerals.
This was done through the "long deeds," wordy documents that gave up
all rights at the going rate—usually fifty cents an acre.

48

The society is still essentially
feudal, still fundamentally composed
of barons and serfs. The distinction
is one of power. The industrialists
—that is, the destroyers and
polluters—are the barons. The serfs
are the millions of one-vote
citizens whose taxes subsidize
and support the system.

This dog's owner was shot
to death when he resisted legalized
strip mining near his home.

49

Following the example set by contractors working for the Tennessee Valley
Authority in Breathitt County, Kentucky, entire mountain ranges will be leveled
layer by layer to recover fuel for steam plants and steel furnaces
and export to Japan.

52

The widow Ollie Combs was arrested here in 1956 when she delayed miners on her property by lying down in front of their bulldozer. The grass in the foreground was planted several years later by the federal government in a vain attempt to reclaim the land.

Widow Combs testifying before the Kentucky legislature.

Three years after strip mining near the author's house.

Industry has always treated the mountains with contempt, and today some
ten thousand miles of streams carry a horrendous freight of silt and sulfuric acid
from unsealed mines. The destroying institutions include the TVA, the major
steel companies, the railroads, and, as always in enterprises of pollution and ruin,
the great names in petroleum. As the American Carthage spreads west, the big
names in strip mining will be Peabody Coal Company, Atlantic Richfield
Company, Garland Coal and Mining Company, Pacific Power and Light Company,
and Consolidated Coal Company.

The owner of this house in Jones Creek, Kentucky, was forced to move when
debris ten feet deep was deposited by his house. This landslide occurred
after Kentucky's highly praised 1966 legislation was passed to limit strip mining.
Law enforcement officials said that strip miners had not violated the law.

CHAPTER III

Strip mining in Kentucky began modestly enough. In 1752, one Christopher Gist was sent by the colonial governor of Virginia on a trip of exploration that took him west as far as the Ohio River. Among the discoveries he reported were the "ledges of fine sea-coal" at many places in the mountains—though neither he nor the governor gave serious thought to exploiting them. Nor did the early settlers, who had fuel enough from the trees they girdled as they cleared the land. As the supply of wood dwindled in the bluegrass section of central Kentucky, entrepreneurs went into the hill country, where they hired a few mountaineers to dig the coal from the shallow beds on the hillsides and along the creeks. Shipped by raft down the Big Sandy and Kentucky rivers, it was sold by the bushel in Louisville, Frankfort, and Lexington to warm the homes of the well-to-do. The poor, then as now, shivered and put on more clothes.

The coal rafts began their trips downriver as early as 1825. The miners, who included black slaves along with white wage laborers, drove tunnels a few dozen yards long into stream banks and loaded the coal into sacks or onto small sleds. Sometimes, with pick and shovel, they would follow an outcropping until the overlay of soil and slate or sandstone would no longer hold up. Thus strip mining made its first appearance in the land explored by Daniel Boone.

Although workmen could not go deeper than a dozen feet into such "opencast" workings, around 1825 a new tool began the series of technological developments that have brought the coal-mining industry to its present state. This tool was a mule-drawn scraper, consisting of a flat-bottomed steel scoop a yard across, with a wooden tilting handle on each side. Attached by a chain to a singletree, it was hitched to a mule and dragged over the ground. A single load would bring away several bushels of earth and loose stones. When the soil had thus been scraped away, exposing the cap rock above the coal, a "churn drill" was used to bore through the rock. A "shaker" sat with the drill between his knees, while a "driver" struck at it with a sledgehammer. After each such blow, the "shaker" lifted the drill and gave it a half-turn, thus sinking it by degrees into the layer of shale or sandstone. When the vein of coal had finally been reached several times over, the holes made by the drill were tamped with black powder, which was set off with a slow-burning fuse. The rock shattered by the explosion was dragged off and piled onto the spoil heaps beside the trench. Then the coal was shoveled onto wagons and hauled off to the rafts.

The quantity of coal shipped downriver remained small until after the Civil War. But the period of industrial growth following the end of that conflict was powered almost entirely by coal. By the 1880s, with the recognition that title to the coal beds could open the way to a profitable operation, land-buying agents began coming into the Appalachian region with offers of gold and greenbacks for land. The people they found there had now been isolated by the lack of roads for nearly a century. Few of the men, and almost none of the women, had ever traveled as far from home as the county seat. Schools were so few that only about 10 percent could write their names, and perhaps half of those were functionally illiterate.

The ordinary mountaineer lived in a one- or two-room cabin and worked the soil for subsistence, eating salt pork, cornmeal, beans, and whatever eggs and milk a few chickens and a cow or two were able to provide. Often he operated a still somewhere in the woods, and some of the potent moonshine he made was sold downriver at a profit. He cut logs for timber, and occasionally dug ginseng or other herbs for sale. Money was scarce in any event. The reports that a railroad might one day be built into the Appalachians were generally dismissed as a tale not to be believed.

So, when the agents came, the mountain people signed the deeds. Few of them consulted a lawyer beforehand; of those available, most were already in the employ of the purchasing agents. Literally thousands of signatures were affixed to deeds by persons who could not read a word, let alone the pages of fine print in covenants that bound the sellers and their "heirs, successors and assigns forever." The price per acre generally ran from ten cents to half a dollar.

Sometimes title to the land was bought in fee. Sometimes the deed conveyed title to "all coal, oil, gas, stone, salt and salt water, iron, ores and all minerals and metallic substances whatsoever," reserving to the seller the right to continue to use—and pay taxes on—its surface. But the astute Philadelphia lawyers who drafted the deeds that the agents carried in their saddlebags also inserted a clause vesting the buyer and his successors in title with the right to do "any and all things necessary, or by him deemed necessary or convenient in mining and removing the coal" and other minerals. Just to be safe, a further clause granted the owner of the minerals immunity from lawsuits for damages arising out of the extractive process. By the time the last of the deeds had been executed, all but about 6 percent of the mineral wealth of the region was the property of corporations headquartered in New York, Philadelphia, Pittsburgh, Baltimore, Cincinnati—and London. That meager 6 percent was, moreover, of inferior quality and inaccessibly located. Thus it was that the builders of major American corporations—and of vast private fortunes, notably that of the Mellon family—made eastern Kentucky and the coal regions of six neighboring states into a vast colonial preserve. Without fear of illegality, the boards of directors could proceed to exploit the central Appalachians with the same ruthless drive for profit as was being done by other U.S. corporations in Asia, Africa, and Latin America. By the beginning of World War I, the Appalachian highlanders had allowed the control of their destiny to slip into the hands of outsiders. What remained to them was a choice of alternatives: they could stay on as wage slaves to the owners of the mines, or they could emigrate. Many thousands chose the second only after enduring the first.

The hundreds of mines that went into operation between 1910 and 1945 were subterranean, tunneling for miles into the meandering ridges, and shipping out tons of coal by the railroads that were indeed built. But strip mining did not wholly disappear.

As early as 1877, an Otis steam shovel had been set to work peeling away the prairie soil from a coal bed at Pittsburg, Kansas, where a three-foot vein was overlaid with soil and rock to a depth of twelve feet. By 1905, eastern Kentucky saw further developments in this direction as the Lily-Jellico Coal Company opened a mechanical strip mine in Laurel County. Gone were the sweating gangs of men who wielded drills, picks, mattocks, and shovels, or pushed the wheelbarrows; gone were the mules hitched to the jolting scrapers. In their place were the steam drill and the coal-burning Vulcan steam shovel. Mounted on a railroad spur, the shovel lifted more than a cubic yard of coal or spoil at a gulp. And in Europe, meanwhile, light engines that burned oil or gasoline and were far more efficient as well as powerful than their coal-burning forerunners were being developed.

Lewis Mumford has noted the many technological developments that have grown out of mining. They include the railroad, the water pump, the mechanical lift, and systems for artificial lighting and ventilation—all of which were in existence long before the so-called Industrial Revolution. As Mumford points out, "Mining originally set the pattern for later modes of mechanization by its callous disregard for human factors, by its indifference to the pollution and destruction of the neighboring environment. . . . If mining involved speculative economic risks, it also brought huge returns; and this, too, served as a pattern for both capitalist enterprise itself and later mechanization." [1] In our own century, mining has become a race between technologies—those of deep mining on the one hand and of surface mining on the other. Much was to hinge on the competition between the two, and likewise on the competition between coal and other fuels.

During World War II, the federal government subsidized the laying of natural-gas pipelines from the South and Southwest to the fuel-short cities of the Northeast. After the war ended, utility companies continued the expansion of the pipelines, and with astonishing rapidity the long-established monopoly of coal on the space-heating market was broken. During the war the government had also subsidized the development of relatively light and compact oil-burning diesel engines to power ships and electrical installations; soon after the war ended, these engines began to displace the old coal-burning, steam-driven railway locomotives. Oil and gas cornered still other markets while the coal mines were being shut down by a recurring series of nationwide strikes aimed at improving the working conditions and salaries of the miners. By 1952 the coal market had shrunk so drastically that the Appalachian mining companies were in the midst of a depression.

This time, the depression was local rather than nationwide. In the cities, an expanding prosperity meant more jobs, and between 1950 and 1960 entire communities in Appalachia were all but depopulated as men, women, and children climbed into their old cars and headed for a new life in Indianapolis, Cleveland, Detroit, or Chicago. The population of Leslie County, Kentucky, fell from twenty thousand to ten thousand in those ten years; in Harlan County, it dropped from seventy-six thousand

[1] *The Pentagon of Power* (New York, 1970), page 147.

to thirty-five thousand. Few of the young men or women ever returned. The exodus of the educated young was nearly total. Suddenly, nearly all the people left in the hills were the old and disabled, the helpless and hopeless.

The consequences of this draining away of the young and strong were political as well as social. Among those who remained out of the thousands of families made idle by the mechanization of a dwindling coal industry, the proportion who could or would not fend for themselves amounted to a third of the entire remaining population. Welfare rolls, commodity food doles, and makeshift public works became the prime support of these unfortunates. Having ceased to be self-supporting, they were now the wards of bureaucrats and the pawns of increasingly ruthless political machines. Independence counted for little at the polls among those who feared that a wrong vote might bring loss of subsistence—and the machines that delivered the vote were, not surprisingly, more finely attuned to the concerns of the mine operators and the land companies whose holdings they worked than to the needs of the voters whose lives they controlled.

The men whom the machines sent to the state legislature were likewise attuned to the interests of the mining industry. They constructed a revenue system that had no scruples about ordinary citizens but that tenderly exempted the purchases of the coal companies. Thus, for example, a 5 percent retail sales tax was passed that applied to a dental drill but not to a coal auger, to a miner's shovel but not to a twenty-ton mechanical loader capable of lifting more than fifty shovelsful at one swoop and priced at $100,000.

Even more oppressive, if less direct, was what happened to the judiciary, on whom the example was clearly not lost. In the earlier days of the mining industry, a population that had learned to be suspicious had also learned the uses of litigation. Hundreds of suits had reached Kentucky's highest tribunal, the Court of Appeals of Frankfort, calling in question the legal authority of the mining corporations to withdraw the coal from the hills by means injurious to the surface and to the inhabitants of the land. The actions involved the piling of shale and other waste in culm heaps, the polluting and diversion of subterranean and surface waters, the pollution of the air from the burning of culm heaps, and the subsidence of the ground in the wake of mining operations. While the mountaineers were still relatively numerous and assertive, judges and legislators had taken note of their claims, and the decisions brought at least a rough approximation of justice.

State judges in Kentucky, as in nearly all state courts, are elected by popular vote. Thus, by the nature of things, they tend to be politicians first and arbiters of justice after that. Appellate judges in seven of the state's districts are elected to office; in order to remain there, they tend to write opinions consonant with the interests and prejudices of a majority of the voters. This being so, there is little wonder that up until the end of World War II the justices consistently showed some concern for the citizens of the coal-bearing regions of the state.

Thus, for example, the general rule was observed that the owner of mining rights had no authority to impose more damage on the surface than was "reasonable" in the mining and marketing of minerals underlying it.[2] Similarly the court ruled that where copperas-polluted water escaping from a mine had been carried by a stream onto a farm, the farmer could recover damages even without proof of negligence. Thus the mining firms were made insurers against such mishap.[3] Again, it was declared to be the supreme law of the state that the owner of the surface had an "absolute" right to enjoy his land without subsidence brought on by the removal of coal pillars. The owner of the minerals was held liable in damages for such harm to the overlying fields and forests even if the actual mining had been done by another company.[4] The bench sought, as well, to protect the lives of citizens

[2] General Refractories Co. vs. Swetman (303 Ky. 427, 197 S.W. 2nd 908).
[3] Beaver Dam Coal Co. vs. Daniel (227 Ky. 423, 13 S.W. 2nd 254).
[4] Nisbet vs. Lofton (211 Ky. 487, 277 S.W. 828); North-East Coal Co. vs. Hayes (244 Ky. 639, 51 S.W. 2nd 960).

with rulings that failure to protect the mouth of a shaft with safety gates rendered the company liable to persons injured while on the premises.[5] Tailings and debris from mines had to be scattered across various surface tracts in reduced heaps so as to minimize injury to any one owner, as a matter of "ordinary and common convenience."[6]

But in the years after World War II, a new and pitiless line of decisions followed the introduction of large-scale strip mining. The first such case was Russell Fork Coal. vs. Hawkins,[7] brought up on appeal from the Circuit Court of Pike County. After the operator had ripped all the vegetation from twelve acres of extremely steep land at the head of a creek, a flash flood—a common phenomenon in the Appalachians—tumbled a mass of mining spoil into the swollen stream. Though by a miracle no lives were lost, the flood swept all the houses in the valley before it. A number of suits for damages brought substantial verdicts in favor of the victims, whereupon the company took its case to the more sympathetic tribunal at Frankfort. The decision of the state judges in effect declared that the masses of soil, the uprooted trees, and the slabs of rock and slate had been harmless until set in motion by the force of water. It was nature that had unleashed the water; thus the damage to the plaintiffs was solemnly declared to be an act of God—for which no coal operator, God-fearing or otherwise, could be held responsible. The ruling absolved the stripper of all damages and sent his hapless victims onto the welfare rolls.

A year after the Russell Fork Coal Company had been adjudged blameless, the same court took up the complaint of a farmer that the stream flowing through his property had been contaminated by a discharge of waste petroleum from an oil well.[8] Ac-

[5] Mosely's Administrators vs. Black Diamond Coal Co. (33 Ky. Rep. 110, 109 S.W. 306).

[6] Blue Diamond Coal Co. vs. Eversole (253 S.W. 2nd 850)) .

[7] 311 Ky. 449, 223 S.W. 2nd 887.

[8] Carver vs. Tanner (312 Ky. 388, 227 S.S. 2nd 905).

cording to its finding, no "material damage" had been done to the farmer, since the discharge merely increased the flow of water in the stream; moreover, it was noted, an injunction against such drainage would have caused "substantial injury" to the oil driller. The case was dismissed, and the costs were borne by the farmer.

As late as the year 1946, the Kentucky state court strongly implied that strip mining was so devastating to the surface that it could not legally be employed if another method of recovering the coal was feasible.[9] Seven years later, the court had evidently had a change of heart. In Buchanan vs. Watson [10] the court dealt squarely for the first time with the conflict between the mineral-owning company and its strip-mining lessee, on the one hand, and the owner of the surface who wanted his property left undisturbed, on the other. The trial judge ruled that the company, since it owned the coal, had the right to extract its property by any means it might choose, but was bound to pay in full for the damage to the surface. The company appealed, seeking authority to ruin the surface without incurring liability—an authority no one but a robber or a coal baron would expect to obtain. The justices handed down an opinion sustaining the claim of the farmer to just remuneration for his loss. The company then petitioned for a rehearing; and during the weeks that followed, in the words of one statehouse watcher, "coal company and railroad lawyers and lobbyists were as thick around the Capitol as horseflies on a mule's back." The buzzing of this swarm had its effect, and the original opinion was withdrawn. The astonishing new conclusion, that the owner of the surface had no grounds for complaint when bulldozers uprooted trees, plowed up pastures, or demolished fences on his property, was based on two considerations, neither of which would appear to have any connection with law or equity; first, that the land destroyed was of relatively little value, and second, that since the coal industry was not unduly prosperous at the time, a decision against the company "would

[9] Treadway vs. Wilson (301 Ky. 702, 192 S.W. 2nd 949).
[10] 290 S.W. 2nd 40.

create great confusion and much hardship in a segment of an industry that can ill afford such a blow."

Thus the highest court of the State of Kentucky boldly and arrogantly based a landmark decision on considerations that were patently economic. The implications of that decision for the bituminous coal industry, and no less for the people and the land of the coal-bearing mountain region, were profound. Having thus been given sanction, stripping flourished as never before. Subterranean mine operators could not compete with the strippers, and as their operations were abandoned, the miners who had lost their jobs became part of the exodus to the cities. Farmers driven off their land moved into the coal towns vacated by the miners, and the relief rolls grew. The one cheerful note in all the gloom was that, thanks to the strippers, cheap coal flooded the market, and the price remained stable for a decade. Nor were the strip miners the only beneficiaries; there were also the electric power companies, and above all there was the TVA.

CHAPTER IV

Possibly the most original American statesman the twentieth century has yet produced was George William Norris of Nebraska. Born in Indiana, this "fighting liberal" led a series of important and wide-ranging crusades throughout a public career that spanned four decades. In the successive roles of prosecuting attorney, judge, Congressman and U.S. Senator, he was tireless as an advocate of enlarged opportunity for people generally and an end to special privilege for a few. Hated by the same corporate managers who branded Franklin D. Roosevelt a traitor and communist, he shaped legislative programs enabling farmers to fend off bankruptcy, to make Congress more amenable to the popular will, to conserve natural resources, and to promote the public ownership of electric power.

The capstone of Norris's career was the Tennessee Valley Authority. The basin of the turbulent Tennessee River had been desolated by the ruinous agricultural practices of more than a century. During World War I, a shortage of nitrates—required in manufacturing TNT—led Congress to authorize the construction of a dam and two nitrogen-fixation plants a few miles below Muscle Shoals in Alabama, a shallow, boulder-strewn stretch where the river fell 130 feet over a distance of thirty-seven miles. With the end of the war came a bitter controversy over the dam and its power-generating turbines and transmission lines. A series of bills introduced by Senator Norris, providing for their operation by the government, was passed by Congress but vetoed by two Republican Presidents. Then came the New Deal, and the Tennessee Valley Authority Act became law—a sweeping program of conservation and reform measures, both political and social, aimed at rescuing a broad subregion out of its self-perpetuating squalor and poverty. The series of dams to be constructed under the Authority would rein the unmanageable Tennessee and its tributaries, at the same time providing vast quantities of hydro-electric power. These installations, together with the nitrate plants, would take advantage of cheap and abundant labor in making available cheap fertilizer along with cheap power and an abundance of water to the stricken valley. In its early years, the project fulfilled the expectations of those who designed it and who managed it—including Arthur Morgan, the Authority's first chairman, and his successor David Lilienthal. The valley prospered as one after another of the great dams and their generators were completed. The river was indeed tamed, and the eroded hills were reclaimed and made green and fertile once again. Capital from the East and from abroad went into the building of plants for the manufacture of textiles, synthetic fibers, paper, and furniture, among scores of other products. Within a decade the valley of the Tennessee had become the showpiece of the nation. The first of the great dams was named for George Norris. When he died in 1944, he had reason to believe that this monument to his career was the forerunner of similar federal authorities throughout the United States.

During World War II, the TVA's massive generators made possible a development never anticipated by Senator Norris—the secret research at the Oak Ridge Gaseous Diffusion Plant that played an important role in producing the atomic bomb. Thus a project begun for the purpose of supplying TNT had come full circle with an infinitely more powerful explosive. Without the enormous supplies of electrical power made available by the TVA, in a time when power shortages occasionally darkened entire cities, the project headed by General Leslie Groves would hardly have been possible.

By the time the war ended, it was evident that the cycle of rejuvenation launched by the Authority had succeeded almost too well. Coal and oil furnaces were junked as more and more homeowners switched to electric heat. As electrical appliances, from refrigerators to hair dryers, became commonplace in more and more households, and new factories proliferated in the vicinity of Kingsport, Knoxville, and Nashville, the Authority discovered that it had opened up a demand for electricity greater than it had waterpower to supply. So, as a supplemental source of power, it turned to coal.

"Cheap power" was now an obsession with the TVA. One after another, ten coal-fired generators were built to produce it. Of the ninety-nine billion kilowatt hours produced annually by the agency, at a value of $388 million, 80 percent are now derived from coal. As the nation's largest single consumer of coal, in 1968 it burned about 5.5 percent of the country's entire output, amounting to one thousand six hundred carloads a day. Half of this amount comes from strip mines. Inevitably, for good or ill, TVA now controls the fate of the coal-bearing regions of Appalachia —setting market trends, changing or fixing prices, controlling the development of mining technology, and in effect prescribing the standards to which a whole spectrum of industries is to adhere. In eastern Kentucky, as elsewhere in central Appalachia, its role has been nothing short of disastrous. The same cheap fuel that made possible an era of prosperity in the TVA region has wrecked the coalfields, impoverished entire communities, and forced thousands of mountain people to desert the place of their birth, leaving behind the graves of countless miners needlessly killed while still others were being crippled for life.

From the time when the purchasing of coal began, the agency's directors have taken the position that they were duty bound to obtain coal at the lowest possible price and without concern for the manner in which it was extracted. That absence of concern led directly to actions that could reduce fuel prices to below prevailing market levels. To ensure a dependable supply of coal, the Authority requested bids on enormous quantities to be delivered over a period of several years. Given the depressed market of the 1950s, competition for the bids was intense, while scores of mines were closing for lack of orders. Thus the nation's largest single consumer found itself operating in a glutted buyer's market. In such a situation, it might have offered a fair and reasonable price as a matter of public policy, which would in turn have tended to stabilize prices and halt the deteriorating effect of low prices within the coal industry. A decent price might have made for reasonable wages, and continuance of union membership for the miners would then have been a matter of course. An insistence on high quality in the coal produced would also have meant deep mining and washeries, with less damage to the environment. But the TVA had lost interest in quality. Its colossal furnaces were equipped to consume coal of a relatively low grade, through a burning process abetted by vastly augmented drafts. Thus, in effect, the coal was bought by the BTU (British thermal unit) rather than by the ton. Coal, shale, and slate went into the flames together, and the remaining ash that did not escape into the atmosphere was compacted into building blocks and road aggregates—an innovation that played further havoc with the economy of the coalfields.

The routine followed by the TVA's purchasing agents was generally as follows: the industry would be asked to submit bids for a specified tonnage of coal of a designated quality, to be delivered over a specified period of time. Typically, fifteen million tons analyzing at thirteen thousand BTUs might be the required quantity over a four-year period. Desperate for orders, the mining companies would hasten to submit bids, calculating every item of the cost with care and offering the fuel at the lowest price consistent with their overhead. When the bids were opened, the lowest offered price would be accepted on only a small portion of the desired tonnage. The bid prices would then be released to the press and the trade journals. Soon new bids would be requested, and the operators would compete in submitting prices still lower than the bid that had been accepted. Throughout the decade beginning in 1955, such procedures were carried through with such effectiveness that the price of steam coal was depressed from about $4.80 to $2.50 per ton. Even the profit-motivated power corporations appeared less greedy, in that they routinely paid a little more for coal than the TVA.

In the Appalachians, most of the subterranean operations lost out in the scramble of bidding for TVA contracts. T. N. Bethell, a Harvard man and Bostonian who came to Appalachia in the fall of 1963, has traced the unsavory history of the relations of the United Mine Workers with the coal companies in the later years of John L. Lewis:

Among the scramblers was the West Kentucky Coal Company, a substantial operation with mines in three states. West Kentucky had resisted the UMW's organizing drives for half a century, and by 1950 . . . the company was something of an embarrassment to Lewis. At some point—the details of time and circumstance are not yet entirely clear—Lewis got together with Cyrus Eaton, the multi-millionaire Cleveland industrialist and board chairman of the Chesapeake and Ohio Railroad. With UMW funds loaned to Eaton on Lewis's authority, Eaton began buying stock in West Kentucky in a strategy to take over the company. By 1952, Eaton was on West Kentucky's board of directors. The following year he became chairman of the board. His first official act as chairman was to sign a wage contract with the UMW.

By taking control of West Kentucky, the UMW was able to move into the huge new TVA market—and huge it was: between 1951 and 1956, while the coal market as a whole remained fairly static, TVA increased its annual purchases from one million to 18 million tons and became the largest single consumer of coal in the world. Through a series of low bids, Eaton and the UMW eventually landed more than 16 percent of the TVA business for West Kentucky Coal Company. . . .

Throughout the 1950's, eastern Kentucky mining, largely carried on by a few major captive mines and a considerable number of relatively small commercial producers, had lagged behind the national average both in productivity and in profits. By the time the industry was hit by a general recession in 1958, the commercial operations in the area were already tending to polarize between a few efficiently mechanized companies like South-East and a growing number of small, fly-by-night, non-union companies, employing handfuls of men, mining poor seams of coal at marginal profits, ignoring safety regulations, and going out of business with awesome frequency—sometimes reappearing under other names, sometimes simply disappearing when the operators took what little they could keep and left for Florida. In the general area where South-East operates, a total of 33 rail mines were at work in 1949; 10 years later there were six. The rest of the mines, too small to warrant rail service at their portals, were served by trucks.

The 1958 recession hit eastern Kentucky harder than it did the rest of the country, and lasted longer. Coal production dropped 18 percent nationwide between 1957 and 1961; the drop was 30 percent in eastern Kentucky. . . .[1]

So strip mines multiplied as "TVA companies," whose dependence on the agency was virtually total, acquired leases from the holding companies and began dismembering mountains for the coal they contained. They were hardly even mining concerns, except in the loosest meaning of the word. In actuality, rather, they were earthmovers with all the huge and sophisticated machinery of road building at their disposal. The deep miner, even when equipped with the latest electrical devices, simply could not

[1] T. N. Bethell, "Conspiracy in Coal," *The Washington Monthly* (Vol. I, No. 2, March 1969), 65–67.

compete with them in the race for output and profit. Subterranean mining is far less damaging to the land, of course, and its ravages can be reduced still further when Congress chooses to assert the authority vested in it to regulate the process. But there are few champions of the land in the coalfields, and the contempt shown for it by the TVA remains a mockery of the conservationist vision of George Norris.

Year by year, the proportion of strip-mined coal used by the onetime "conservation" agency rose. By 1961, the TVA's suppliers were digging 122 million tons a year, of which 18.5 million tons were bought by the agency and another 56 million by other power producers. Already twenty-five thousand acres had been stripped for the benefit of TVA. In the same year, taking note of a rising chorus of complaints by conservationists, its board of directors began preparing what they modestly described as "an appraisal of Coal Strip Mining." Issued in 1963, it conceded that stream pollution and soil erosion did follow the bulldozers, that stripping lowered land values and made the landscape "unsightly"— but argued that the land itself was of little value, bringing only a few dollars an acre when offered for sale, producing an annual growth of timber worth a mere $8.50 per acre, whereas the same land might yield coal valued at $9,000 to the acre when given over to the shovels and draglines of the strippers. Thus, it was explained, we must simply accept stripping as a part of our national experience. Once again to quote Lewis Mumford, "Only our present one-sided system of bookkeeping, which takes account only of profits, surfeits, and benefits, and ignores environmental damages and human deficits, could have so long remained oblivious to the massive miscarriages of the power system." [2] Thus it is not surprising that the report found little initiative for reclamation among landowners. Though granting that "reclamation" might be achieved at a cost of no more than three cents for each ton of coal extracted, the conclusion was that the matter was one requiring action by the states. The assertion that federal

[2] *The Pentagon of Power* (New York, 1970).

concern was not required simply amounted to an echo of the spokesmen for the coal, rail, and power industries throughout the nation.

Late in 1963, when the poverty of Appalachia appeared, at least for a time, to have become a matter of concern to the Kennedy Administration, Aubrey J. Wagner, chairman of the board of the TVA—"which," it was noted in a dispatch to *The New York Times*, "is regarded by many as the prime example of a successful Federal assault on poverty"—told the press "that cheap T.V.A. power was vital to the whole Appalachian region." How far that region was from benefiting by the kind of assault to which it was then being subjected had been indicated in a front-page story by Homer Bigart in *The New York Times* for October 1, 1963:

. . . Hellier, once a flourishing trading center for surrounding coal camps on Marrowbone Creek, was left stranded three years ago when the Blue Diamond Coal Company abruptly closed the mines and demolished the coke ovens. The mineral rights were sold to a subsidiary of Bethlehem Steel, which decided to extract coal from the other side of the mountain. The bewildered citizens of Hellier felt they were being punished by the coal company because of labor disputes. . . . At Lynch, in Harlan County, one-third of the city is being demolished by United States Coal and Coke, a subsidiary of the U.S. Steel Corporation. . . . The company had strip-mined the steep slopes of Big Black Mountain behind the town. Deprived of the protective cover of forest, the mountainside is exposed to erosion. Last March part of the town was inundated by mud slides that ruined homes and company facilities and choked Looney Creek. . . .

Nor had the situation changed for the better after three years, despite a flurry of Federal concern and the announcement of President Johnson's War on Poverty. According to Ben A. Franklin in *The New York Times* for July 1, 1965,

. . . One strip-mining company here, which already has 30 miles of exposed mountaintop high wall, has just received a 15-year, 37.5-

million-ton contract from the Tennessee Valley Authority. The company will buy $112.5 million worth of coal from the Knott County mountainsides at the rate of 50,000 tons a week, enough to fill 10 trains of 200 hopper cars each.

T.V.A. officials say strip mining is inevitable and would occur even if the Federal power agency were not a major factor in the coal market. It is the single largest purchaser of coal in the country. . . .

Mrs. Bige Ritchie, a hill woman from the head of Sassafras Creek, said when she saw a strip mine bulldozer uproot the coffin of her infant son from the backyard family cemetery and pitch it down the mountainside, "I like to lose my mind over it."

That was about five years ago, and she and her husband, a retired underground miner, did nothing about it. Mrs. Ritchie told her story for the first time at a recent mass meeting of the Appalachian Group to Save the Land and the People, a citizens' committee organized on June 8 by two Kentucky school teachers from the Clear Creek area of Knott County. . . .

It is here that Dan Gibson, the eighty-year-old coffinmaker who had lived all his life in Knott County, enters the story. In the spring of 1965, strippers under contract to extract coal for the TVA reached the tract of land in Clear Creek Valley where Dan and his wife lived. Title to the land—for which mining rights were held by the Kentucky River Coal Corporation—was in the name of Dan's stepson, who was then serving in Vietnam with the Marine Corps. Neither the stepson, his mother, nor Dan himself had authorized the entry of the bulldozers on the property. As they crossed its boundary, the old man picked up his .22-caliber rifle, walked up the hill to meet the invaders, and proceeded to sit down in their path with the rifle cocked and laid across his knee. The events that followed had an element of comic opera, but behind them was an issue of the gravest importance.

When Dan told the visitors that the land was owned by a man fighting for his country "over the waters," and that they had no business ruining his land while he was not there to attend to affairs, the argument—combined with the rifle—raised sufficient question that the workmen, having conferred, withdrew to report to their employers.

But the officials of the Kentucky River Coal Corporation were unwilling to submit to the audacity of a lone old man. Having obtained warrants charging him with breach of the peace and threatening with a deadly weapon, they soon had three cars, carrying nine or ten well-armed sheriff's deputies and state policemen, on their way toward Honey Gap, a low saddle in the mountain not far from where Dan had made his stand. In the meantime his neighbors had assured him that they would take up his cause, and "Uncle Dan" offered no resistance to the enforcement officers who, panting from the climb but flushed with satisfaction, were able to report that they had restored law and order to Clear Creek.

Soon after dawn the next day, the bulldozers were back. And this time they were met not by one old man but what one of the company's lawyers was later to describe as "a big gang of outlaws" —nearly all of them elderly, some of them women—who took up positions at the boundary line and refused to stand aside. A couple of firearms were in evidence, and some threats were audible. Again the engines idled for a few moments before being turned off while their operators departed to report this new development.

What was truly new about it was that several hundred mountain men and women, living in one of the remotest and most primitive of Appalachian communities, had been stirred to action by the realization that their culture, their way of life, and their long connection with the land were in danger. At a time when most of the highlanders had long ago surrendered to apathy, the inhabitants of Clear Creek Valley, and along with them those of several nearby communities, had resolved to fight.

Thus it was that the Appalachian Group to Save the Land and People was born. Fanning out over the countryside in their battered sedans and pickup trucks, they recruited more than a thousand members. Even a few county officials, sensing that there were votes to be won or lost on the issue, decided to join. A chemistry teacher, Leroy Martin, was elected chairman of the group; but Dan Gibson continued to be its main rallying force. There was a meeting at the Knott County Courthouse in Hindman, where to shouts of approval Dan declared, "We are dead certain not going to let them come on to our land and tear it up. We will do whatever it takes to stop the strip miners."

One of the group's first moves was to hire a lawyer, who paid a visit to Governor Edward Breathitt at Frankfort to ask for a meeting with its representatives. At first the governor demurred. Enforcement of the state's reclamation laws would, he said, prevent "undue damage." Besides, he appeared to be uneasy at the thought of a horde of mountaineers descending upon the capitol, where they might, as he put it, "scare my office girls." But after reassurances by the attorney that no stenographer's safety would be endangered, a date was set for the meeting.

At dawn on a bright day late in June, a strange motorcade set out on the 180-mile journey to the state capital. Consisting of ten- and twelve-year-old Plymouths, Fords, and Chevrolets, battered Jeeps and pickup trucks, and including a couple of log carriers, it stretched for nearly a mile along the winding mountain roads. The vehicles had all been washed for the occasion, and the occupants wore the best clothes they had; for many of the women, this meant the old-style homemade dresses Appalachian women have worn for generations. Many of the men were former coal miners, long disabled by black lungs or emphysema. Some were farmers. Many were people on public assistance. Since a number had never before been out of the mountains, it is no wonder that they were more than a little awed by what they had undertaken.

Upon arriving at Frankfort, they stood waiting on the steps of the capitol, a group of eighty or ninety anxious and bewildered but determined petitioners. Upon being told that the governor was in conference, and so busy that he would probably not be able to meet with them, but would send an aide to hear their story, a groan went up. It was Ben Franklin of *The New York Times* who saved the day by pointing out to the governor the unfortunate effect a refusal to see them could have on public relations. The governor reconsidered, and the entire delegation was led to an auditorium where for three hours he and several top assistants listened to their pleas for action by the state to save their land from the bulldozers.

Governor Breathitt, to his credit, was profoundly affected by what he heard. A few days later he flew to Knott County, where he was shown the remains of the family cemetery where Mrs. Ritchie had seen her infant son's coffin disinterred. The results were reported as follows in a United Press International dispatch on July 1, 1965:

> Governor Edward T. Breathitt announced today steps he would take to combat the damage done by strip and auger mining. After a dusty two-hour tour of Knott County, the Governor said: "My visit impressed upon me the urgent need for these actions to be taken at this time."
>
> First, he said, he would ask the Kentucky Attorney General to intervene as a friend of the court in cases attacking the interpretation of "broad-form deeds." . . . The Governor declared he would seek an early conference with the TVA board to discuss its coal-purchasing policies. . . . Governor Breathitt also said he would ask the Kentucky Department of Natural Resources to prepare a regulation controlling strip-mining on precipitous slopes. . . .

In unmistakable terms, the governor gave notice to the coal operators that he was taking up the cause of conservation: "We do not intend to permit this industry, or any other industry, to destroy the beauty of Kentucky's countryside or the usefulness of its earth for future generations." Similarly, he spoke out on the policies of the TVA, after noting the announcement that nearly $53 million from its operations in fiscal 1965 were being returned to the federal treasury. According to a report by Ben A. Franklin in *The New York Times* for July 4, 1965, he declared that "while it is commendable that T.V.A. can operate with such efficiency that it can make a payment of this magnitude . . . I would like to suggest that perhaps some of this revenue should have been spent to help reclaim land which was wrecked in Kentucky and other states to mine T.V.A. coal. . . . I do not believe that any company can be applauded for returning money to the Government simply because it has failed to do its job and because it has neglected the people it has been set up to serve."

To this the TVA, through chairman of the board Aubrey J. Wagner, was quick to respond. Its position was now that "all strip mined lands must be restored—not just those supplying T.V.A.'s needs" and "that unless all states having the problem act quickly, Federal regulation must be the answer."[3] But how little the fundamental position of the agency had changed was clear from a later statement by its Reclamation Director, James Curry. "Strip mining is part of the American way," he said—and then quickly amended the phrase to "an integral aspect of the American economy."[4] It was a view that chairman Wagner obviously shared. In June 1965 he had burbled to Ben Franklin of the *Times:* "Strip mining, while it is going on, looks like the devil, but . . . if you look at what these mountains were doing before this stripping, they were just growing trees that were not even being harvested!"

[3] Letter to *The New York Times,* July 14, 1965.
[4] Gene L. Mason, "The Subversive Poor," *The Nation,* December 30, 1968.

CHAPTER V

To the end of his term, Edward Breathitt upheld the cause of defending the land against the strippers so far as he was able. By canceling the stripping permit on the entire watershed of Clear Creek, he saved—at least for the time being—the land Dan Gibson and his neighbors had taken action to defend. So far as was legally possible, he used executive order to strengthen reclamation requirements—as in the decree that no stripping was to be carried out on land with a gradient steeper than twenty-five degrees. He encouraged state enforcement officers to deny permits where stripping would "directly imperil" homes or other structures. What was needed, of course, was a total ban on stripping in Appalachia; but this, because of the power of the industry, the venality of the legislators, and the unconcern of Kentuckians generally, proved beyond his power.

Late in November 1965, near the town of Hindman, a little gnomelike woman known to her neighbors as the Widow Combs sat down in front of a bulldozer to save her four-room house from destruction. For this bold act she was declared in contempt of court and spent Thanksgiving in jail. The governor intervened by canceling the mining permit of the Caperton Coal Company, and her land—in the shadow of a lovely dark ridge above Honey Gap, so named for the prevalence of wild bees—was saved from the bulldozers.

Meanwhile, the Appalachian Group to Save the Land and People had been putting together a legal defense fund as a necessary step toward obtaining redress through the courts. Brought up on a nineteenth-century confidence in "the law" as based on reason and justice, they refused to believe that any branch of their government could be entirely under the sway of special economic interests. At meetings in stark little churches, sagging school-houses, or cramped cabins, their spokesmen appealed for dona-tions to the fund, and the gnarled, work-hardened hands dropped crumpled dollar bills, one by one, into Dan Gibson's hat. Women brought in painfully accumulated savings from the sale of eggs and honey that had been "laid by" against illness or a visit someday to a son who had moved away. In some endangered communities, there were bake sales or sewing bees to raise money for the fund. Slowly, the dimes and quarters and bills grew to a hoard of three thousand dollars, and the Appalachian Group to Save the Land and People filed suit for a declaratory judgment against the coal companies.

The case, which went first to the circuit court of Knott County, was brought on behalf of LeRoy Martin, the teacher who had been elected chairman of the Appalachian Group. For years he and his wife had saved to build their house, a modest but im-maculate one sparkling with fresh paint and set in a green, well-tended lawn, on a narrow strip of level land at the foot of a timbered hill. On the slope, all the cleared areas had been re-planted to pines and fruit trees. The "mineral estate" on the prop-erty belonged to the Kentucky Oak Mining Company, thanks to a deed of exceptional length and labyrinthine complexity to which in 1903 a mountaineer and his wife, both of them illiterate, had set the marks. Subterranean tunnels had already been driven to work the hidden seams of coal during the 1930s and 1940s; the outcrop, however, remained unworked, and it was rich and tantalizing. To strip it would have ruined the Martins' entire investment; sooner or later a cascade of mud and rubble would have doomed the lawn, the vegetable garden, and the house itself. Whether such considerations could weigh in the scales against the TVA's appetite for cheap coal, and the hunger of all healthy, red-blooded American corporations for profits and more profits, remained the question.

Governor Breathitt prevailed on the attorney general of the state to assign one of his young assistants to help in preparing the case. Prior decisions by the State Court of Appeals that authorized stripping without the consent of the owner, it was argued in the petition, had been in error for a number of reasons: (a) stripping had been unheard of by the sellers when the broad-form deeds were executed and thus could not have been contemplated by the parties to these transactions; (b) in the intervening years the owners of the mineral deposits had permitted surface owners to make valuable improvements which would be wrecked by stripping, and were thereby estopped from that form of mining; (c) the tools and techniques of present-day strip mining had not been invented at the time the deeds were executed, and their employment necessarily introduced a degree of destructiveness never endorsed by the sellers of the mineral rights; and (d) stripping is so irremediably destructive of the physical environment as to rule out continued human residence on the land and is therefore in violation of sound public policy and accordingly unlawful.

None of these arguments was in any way novel or original. They had been sustained in the highest courts of Ohio, Indiana, Illinois, West Virginia, Virginia, Pennsylvania, and Colorado. Kentucky was urged to apply the relatively humane case law of other coal-producing states in situations where the owners of underlying minerals sought to tear them out of the earth without the permission of the owners of the topsoil and without consideration of the effect of the operation on plants and animals.

In due time the circuit judge rendered an opinion that neatly straddled the issue. He ruled that the coal operator had the right at law to engage in strip mining but must pay fair and full compensation for all harm inflicted on the surface. Both sides promptly appealed.

An overwhelming majority of the landowners in the coalfields of eastern Kentucky are descendants of men who fought in the Revolutionary War. They think of themselves as freeholders—a concept that simply loses its meaning wherever one property owner finds himself absolutely at the mercy of another. It is a supremely bitter irony that a generation sprung from the victors of King's Mountain, whose land titles often trace back to grants issued as compensation for service in that and other campaigns, should now find themselves defenseless against corporations contracted to dig coal for an agency of the United States government.

Every pertinent principle of law and equity was argued with skill in the Court of Appeals. Briefs Amicus Curiae were filed on behalf of the Martins and all others in a similar plight by lawyers for the Sierra Club and the Kentucky Civil Liberties Union, as well as the Appalachian Group to Save the Land and People and the Commonwealth of Kentucky. In support of the industry, briefs were filed by counsel for numerous coal companies and for the National Association of Coal Lessors on the question of whether people who reside upon and draw their sustenance from the surface of the earth may lawfully prevent its destruction by corporations digging for coal.

In an opinion handed down on June 21, 1968, by a majority of five out of seven judges, the hopes of the Appalachian Group and its supporters were crushed. Every argument of the coal industry was sustained. In substance, the majority held that the owner of underlying minerals may totally ruin the surface of the earth without the consent of the man who owns and tills it—and without paying him anything for his loss!

Few Kentucky lawyers were surprised by the decision, but among thousands of mountain families it deepened the hopelessness of the old and the cynicism of the young. What comfort was left came from a ringing dissent by Judge Hill—a document that is worth quoting at length:

Martin vs. Kentucky Oak Mining Co.
429 S.W. 2d (Ky.) 395:

Not only is the majority opinion contrary to the laws of sister coal states, such as West Virginia and Pennsylvania, as I shall point out later, but the majority opinion is inconsistent with other opinions of this court in similar situations. This court decided in *Wiser Oil Company v. Conley*, Ky., 346 S.W. 2d 718 (1960), that the owner of oil and gas rights had no right to use the water-flooding method of recovering oil without the consent of the owner of the surface. This Court said in Wiser at page 721:

"Even though appellants assert that the water-flooding process was known prior to March 10, 1917, the date of execution of the lease, and was employed to some extent in other states before that time, *we conclude it was the intention* of the parties that oil should be produced by drilling in the customary manner *that prevailed when the lease was executed.* Any exemption from liability would therefore be limited to the damages which might be caused by this *contemplated* means of bringing oil to the top." [Emphasis added.]

Wiser and Buchanan are as inconsistent as sin and salvation.

I am shocked and appalled that the court of last resort in the beautiful state of Kentucky would ignore the logic and reasoning of the great majority of other states and lend its approval and encouragement to the diabolical devastation and destruction of a large part of the surface of this fair state without compensation to the owners thereof.

Following is a list of some of the cases from six other states that take a view contrary to the majority opinion in the present case. *Franklin v. Callicoat*, Ohio, 119 N.E. 2d 688; *East Ohio Gas Company v. James Brothers Coal Company*, Ohio, 85 N.E. 2d 816; *Williams v.*

Hay, 120 Pa. 485; 14 Atl. 379; *Livingston v. Moingona Coal Company*, 49 Iowa 369, 31 Am. Rep. 150; *Catron v. So. Butte Mining Co.*, 181 Fed. 941, 104 C.C.A. 405; *Oresta v. Romano Brothers*, 137 W.Va. 633, 73 S.E. 2d 622; *West Virginia-Pittsburgh Coal Company v. Strong*, W.Va., 42 S.E. 2d 46; *Rochez Bros., Inc. v. Duricka*, 374 Pa. 262, 97 Atl. 2d 825; *C & O Railroad Company v. Bailey Production Corporation*, 163 F. Supp. 666; *Campbell v. Campbell*, Tenn., 199 S.W. 2d 931; *United States v. Polino*, 131 F. Supp. 772 (N.D. W.Va. 1955); *Wilkes-Barre Township School District v. Corgan*, 403 Pa. 383, 170 A. 2d. 97 (1961); *Rocky Mountain Fuel Co. v. Heflin*, (Colo.) 366 P. 2d 577 (1961); *Benton v. U. S. Manganese Corp.*, 313 S.W. 2d 839 (1958).

I cannot bring myself to the conclusion that it was the intention of the parties at the time the minerals were reserved to permit the owner of the minerals to completely destroy the surface of the farm which is now owned by the defendants.

I confess I think strip mining without proper reclamation procedures is a catastrophe. I consider it against public policy and detrimental to the general welfare of the state, and any contract pertaining thereto is illegal as being against public policy. Of course, where the land is not steep and proper reclamation practices are followed, strip mining may be justified.

The public policy of the state of Kentucky was accurately expressed by the Legislature in KRS 350.020, from which I quote:

"The General Assembly finds that the unregulated strip mining of coal causes soil erosion, stream pollution, the accumulation of stagnant water and the seepage of contaminated water, increases the likelihood of floods, destroys the value of land for agricultural purposes, counteracts efforts for the conservation of soil, water and other natural resources, destroys or impairs the property rights of citizens, creates fire hazards dangerous to life and property, so as to constitute an imminent and inordinate peril to the welfare of the Commonwealth."

I recognize that the regulation of strip mining is not for the courts but for the Legislature. However, I would go further and say as a matter of law that any deed, whether it be "broad form" or otherwise, that attempts to grant strip mining (when the grade is approximately 20 percent or more) is illegal and unenforcible as against public policy and detrimental to the present and succeeding generations.

I freely recognize and respect the rule of *stare decisis*, and I oppose changing rules of law without compelling reasons, but it is wrong and unjust to take the position that once judicial error has gained the respectability of age it becomes somehow invulnerable to correction by the court which made it.

Although the majority opinion relies upon Buchanan and zealously guards its borders on all sides from every change, modification or encroachment, I am able to see a ray of hope in Buchanan which is overlooked, ignored, and disregarded by the majority opinion. This ray of hope is contained in the following quotation from Buchanan, supra, at page 43:

"The owner of the mineral has the paramount right to the use of the surface in the prosecution of its business for any purpose of necessity or convenience, unless this power is exercised *oppressively*, arbitrarily, or maliciously, in which event the surface owner may recover for damages so occasioned."

Webster's Third New International Dictionary defines "oppressive" thus: "unreasonably burdensome; unjustly severe, rigorous, or harsh."

I contend that any major destruction of the surface is "unreasonably burdensome; unjustly severe" and "harsh." But no, the opinion of the majority of this court, as now constituted, would not afford the appellants herein the benefit of the plain and simple meaning of its own precedent. In the interest of consistency, the majority opinion should reform the rule in Buchanan so as to delete the word "oppressive" therefrom and should overrule its opinion in Wiser Oil, then the slate would be clean insofar as the legal status of a few greedy exploiters of the land is concerned.

I would point out that in Buchanan, supra, this court shed great crocodile tears for the coal industry when the opinion said: "To disturb this rule now would create great confusion and much hardship in a segment of an industry that can ill afford such a blow." Obviously the court was grieving for the coal industry. Instead of helping the coal industry, the rule in Buchanan really hurt it by helping a few strip and auger operators. It was said in *Kentucky Law Journal*, volume 50, number 4, page 529, that: "Contrary to the implication of the court's conclusion, Buchanan helped the holding companies more than the 'industry.' "

Thus Kentucky gave forthright legal sanction to terracide, a crime that many Americans loudly deplore and many others eagerly commit.

While the case of *Martin vs. Kentucky Oak Mining Co.* was making its way through the courts, the mountaineers were resorting to guerrilla tactics against the strip-mining companies. In the summer of 1967, a diesel-powered shovel valued at $50,000 was blown up by nocturnal raiders at the Kentucky Oak Company's stripping site in Knott County. On August 6 of the same year, $300,000 worth of machinery owned by the Tar Heel Coal Company was blown up on Lost Creek. Using carbon nitrate, the demolitionists destroyed a $90,000 auger, a D-9 bulldozer valued at $84,000, two trucks, two drills, and a welder. So many rifle bullets were fired at the machines on Lost Creek that some of the bulldozers were given armor plate and looked more than ever like military tanks. In Bell County, a year later, more than three quarters of a million dollars' worth of equipment was reduced to rubble in a single night. It is no wonder that in Letcher County a local weekly, *The Mountain Eagle,* carried in a single issue the offers of a reward by five different companies for information leading to the arrest and conviction of persons responsible for industrial sabotage—all of it involving explosions.

At the same time, the strip-mining interests were employing tactics of another sort against the efforts of antipoverty workers, specifically those connected with Appalachian Volunteers (AVs) and the Southern Conference Educational Fund (SCEF), to organize the mountain people. In Pike County, as Gene L. Mason tells the story,

Jink Ray, supported by neighbors, AVs and SCEF workers, decided to stand in front of the bulldozer as it was pulling onto his land. He did, and refused to budge; the dozer went away. After a series of legal battles in which the local courts issued injunctions against Ray to prevent his interference with the stripping of his own land, Governor Breathitt came to his aid. He had the strip mine permit of the Puritan Coal Company revoked. Joe Mulloy, an AV and one of Ray's neighbors, said that "the Jink Ray victory had tremendous implications for the poor and working class in Appalachia. This was perhaps the first time since the heyday of the United Mine Workers that the operators had been challenged and defeated by the people. Ray's victory could serve as an inspiration to people all over the mountains to demand and take back what is theirs, the coal. The coal operators knew this all too well."

Meanwhile, the AVs were receiving threatening phone calls in the middle of the night. Then, during the last week of July, 1967, the Pike County Sheriff, a representative of the Small Business Administration, and Robert Holcomb, president of the Pikeville Chamber of Commerce, visited the homes of [Alan] McSurely [an SCEF worker] and Mulloy. They questioned Mulloy generally about what he was doing in Pike County, and specifically about strip mining. Their stay was short but long enough to suggest subtly that they'd better be careful. That evening Holcomb called for a federal investigation of the AVs in Pike County.

Then . . . on August 11, 1967 . . . Alan McSurely's home was invaded by Commonwealth Attorney Thomas Ratliff . . . and fifteen armed deputies. They combed every piece of printed or written material in the home for two hours—especially the research library of the coal industry that the McSurelys had collected—and confiscated all of it. When they discovered that Margaret McSurely had worked for SNCC in 1964, they arrested her as well as her husband. By midnight they had reached Mulloy's home and put him under arrest. . . .

The word began to spread that those arrested were Communists. . . . Ratliff then arrested Carl Braden and his wife Ann, Executive Directors of SCEF, for attempting to overthrow the government of

Pike County. Mrs. Braden had never set foot in the county, and her husband's only appearance there was to get McSurely and Mulloy out on bond.

Under the leadership of William Kunstler of Rutgers' Law Center for Constitutional Rights the anti-poverty workers eventually managed to get the 1920 state sedition act, which they had been charged with violating, declared unconstitutional. . . .

Heavy pressure was put on Governor Breathitt to rid the state of AVs. Breathitt succumbed and recommended to OEO Director Shriver that funds for AVs be cut off. On August 18, 1967, Shriver acted. He cut off the funds without a hearing and without notifying the AV director. Some funds were later reinstated, but the AVs received no new funds from OEO.

A confidential OEO report laid the arrests principally to "obvious political interest." This corroborated an FBI report which stated that Ratliff's prime interest was "ridding Pike County of the anti-poverty workers." It added, "Ratliff's reasons for attacking the program are economic and political: (1) he has made a fortune out of the coal industry and still had coal interests; and (2) he is running for Lt. Governor on the Republican ticket and thinks it is a good issue." But despite an agreement with the three-judge federal court not to act until the court could reach a decision on the constitutionality of the state sedition law, Ratliff proceeded with a Pike County grand jury investigation of the McSurelys and Mulloy. . . . When the Kentucky legislature met in early 1968 legislators swallowed what they were fed by the Pike County power structure. . . . The new Governor, Republican Louis B. Nunn, made a campaign promise to "run SCEF and organizations like it out of the state." To implement his promise, a Kentucky Un-American Activities Committee (KUAC) was established.

So the efforts of a sympathetic governor and the determined resistance of the mountain people were not enough to stop the juggernaut. Mr. Mason quoted Edith Easterling, a longtime resident of Pike County who was active with the Appalachian Volunteers: "You should see the way some of those county officers treat the people in the hollers. A friend of mine went down to the high sheriff's office and wanted to make some complaints because we hadn't been getting any law enforcement. . . . The deputy said she was just a Communist, she works for the AVs; and as long as they were going to be Communist, then they wouldn't have anybody from the sheriff's office going out there." Mrs. Easterling later testified that "some of the people up in the mountains are so scared of the courthouse gang in Pikeville that they haven't been out of their hollers to go to town for twenty years. Most of them are disabled miners with the black lung, and are afraid someone will take their checks."[1] Small wonder, then, that a new pall of hopelessness gradually settled over the whole region of eastern Kentucky.

[1] Gene L. Mason, "The Subversive Poor," *The Nation*, December 30, 1968.

"Mining techniques have changed. It has become a simple matter to reach and remove a seam of coal with a dozen men—instead of hundreds. Automation has made the miner jobless. And as the mines rejected him, so did his union, for which he had picketed, fought, and even died. So the mountaineer became another paradox: an unemployed and unemployable industrial worker in a wilderness setting. . . ."—John Fetterman's *Stinking Creek* (Dutton, 1967).

The Ohio Power Company boasts
of its reclamation project near
Caldwell, Ohio, while trumpeting the
earthmoving capacity of
"Big Muskie."

The Wall Street Journal commented
on May 24, 1971, "many students
of strip mining are convinced that
reclamation of the land currently
being stripped by mammoth
machines is impossible."

Like a prehistoric monster of
death, the hundred-foot-high Gem of
Egypt peels back the soil
"overburden" to reveal a rich seam
of coal in Belmont County, Ohio.

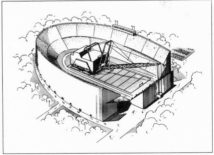

An artist's rendering of
"Big Muskie" in the 81,000-seat
Ohio Stadium at Columbus. The
pride of the American Electric
Power Company is 32 stories high
and weighs 27 million pounds.

A poisoned stream in southeastern Ohio. Silt-laden streams run bright red with iron precipitate or frothy white with sulfur. They are highly acid—even to the point of deteriorating concrete—and fish have forsaken them.

Even bulldozers shrink to insignificance alongside today's mountain-moving
machines. American Metal Climax's forty-yard dragline works a mine
of its subsidiary, Ayrshire Coal Company. Exposed coal seam is shown in the
foreground of the photograph above.

The U.S. Geological Survey's report on strip mining in McCreary County, Kentucky, released April 11, 1971, is a study of ecological devastation. These pictures from the report demonstrate nature's inability to reclaim stripped land. The bottom photograph was taken more than six years after mining had ceased. Only 5 percent of the land stripped in Kentucky has been restored, according to Interior Department figures.

Walls sixty feet high are a reminder of an old strip mine near Beefhide, Kentucky. Boulders the size of automobiles were blasted over the mountainside, forcing many residents to flee their homes.

We have a strange relationship to our land, but our past is without a viable land ethic or any really deep comprehension of the earth. The stripper's only fear is the outrage of all of us to an industry that could suggest, as it did in 1971, that scarred and barren stripped "badlands" could become a tourist attraction.

CHAPTER VI

That Kentucky has a "strip-mining law" ostensibly marks it as a state where comparative enlightenment prevails. Three sessions of the Kentucky General Assembly had attempted to deal with the matter before the bill was finally passed in 1954, over the concerted opposition of the state's coal operators. It has since been amended five times, in a process editorial writers like to refer to as "tightening"—with the result, according to these same gentry, that Kentucky has the "toughest" reclamation law in the nation. Whether this is true seems doubtful; but in any event, as the preceding chapters make clear, its effect on the Appalach‑ ian counties has been negligible. Nevertheless, in a general way the Kentucky law has become the model to be followed by other states—although, as this is written, at least six states in which stripping occurs have no reclamation laws whatever.

I was a member of the Kentucky Legislature in 1954, when the law was passed with the sponsorship of Governor Lawrence Wetherby. The reaction of the coal industry to the proposal was true to the pattern it can be expected to follow whenever govern‑ ment at any level moves to legislate any matter affecting it.

Whether the issue is safety, providing for dependents, or protecting the environment, the spokesmen for the coal industry are ready to howl that the act will (1) impose an "undue burden" on the mining companies; (2) force the operators out of business, thus bringing starvation to whole communities; (3) drive the industry out of the state; (4) saddle the state with the reputation of being antibusiness; (5) kill the goose that lays the golden egg; (6) move the state one step closer to communism or a police dictatorship; and (7) undermine the churches and all the God-fearing little businessmen who depend on the wages of the miners and the mine operators. The spectacle of a vice-president of the Consolidation Coal Company in sharkskin suit and alligator shoes exhorting bemused legislators in this fashion, incredible though it may seem, is simply a fact of life in Frankfort.

In 1954, for all these reasons, I found myself being urged by lobbyists for "Consol," the country's largest coal producer, to vote against the proposed mining regulations. Furthermore, I was told that Consol owned forty thousand acres in the mountains of Kentucky which it had plans to strip—an operation that would encompass five thousand ridge-line miles in five counties, recover millions of tons and pay high wages to a host of honest laborers. At this point, the spokesman for Consol was interrupted by a spokesman for the Elkhorn Coal Corporation whose company had plans to "develop" another twelve hundred ridge-line miles in like fashion, unless prevented from doing so by restrictions enacted at the behest of "a bunch of ignorant do-gooders and conservationists."

Once the law was passed, and after public opinion had flared up briefly now and then over the continuing ravages of strip mining, the coal operators were moved to hire skillful public relations men who now praise the law their lobbyists once branded as oppressive and communistic. At the behest of these new experts carefully manicured and lavishly fertilized demonstration areas have been planted to grass and a few apple trees, which are repeatedly photographed as proof of the industry's tenderness for the environment. Rarely are the requirements of the law so much as adhered to; they are virtually never exceeded.

The statute requires a strip miner to obtain a permit, for which he is charged a fee of fifty dollars, plus twenty-five more for each acre to be "affected." In the place of appropriations, the state's Reclamation Commission is dependent on the fees paid by would-be strippers—a state of affairs that seems calculated to ensure that permits will be issued freely. The stripper, having obtained a permit, must file a map of the area in question, showing its terrain and elevations, and a plan for the reclamation of the land once the coal has been extracted. Such plans may not envisage the dumping of spoil into streams or onto roads. The operator then files a bond amounting to from one hundred to five hundred dollars an acre, under penalty of forfeiture if the plan is not complied with. Once the plan has been approved—as such plans always are, with no more than trifling modifications—the work of "recovering" the coal can begin.

One Kentucky politician has compared these arrangements with the legalizing of rape in cases where the rapist agrees to restore his victim to her original condition. Under these conditions, he mused, "we would get a lot of applications and execute a lot of bonds and a good many females would sure as hell be raped— but restorations would be exceedingly rare." And so it is, indeed, with the land under the Kentucky reclamation law. Concern for the stripped hills becomes a blizzard of letters to editors, of news stories that laud or denounce the industry, of solemn editorial pronouncements, of applications, permits, bonds, maps, reports, bond releases, and so on ad infinitum. And while the paper blizzard swirls and is stacked in ever-growing files, the stripper and his machines go about their glorious work of digging out the coal.

This is the way they work: the scene is a forested ridge, rising a thousand feet above the glistening creek that winds in and out, defining the terrain; at its crest is a "razorback" of sharply exposed rock. Two-thirds of the way up, the forest is composed of second-growth hardwoods interspersed here and there with a few pines. The old "cleared line" is evident where the ancient growth of gnarled oaks, beeches, and gums, standing among moss-grown boulders, replaces the younger trees. On the eroded lower slopes, a remarkable amount of humus has been restored by the annual leaf fall from the tulip trees and other species that make up the second growth. The original complex community—rodents, lizards, hawks and owls, swarms of bees and whole empires of insect societies, the bacteria and the fungi—still carries on the multitudinous self-renewing processes of decay and rebirth.

An echo of the bulldozer's roar reverberates from other hills as the huge blade shears the topsoil, bringing an upheaval of the underlayer of clay and crumbly particles of carbon—the "bloom" from the vein of coal. As the treads of the huge earthmover cut deeper into the ground, the topsoil is flung up in a wave a yard deep. Now the first tree—a fifteen-year-old poplar with a diameter of eight inches, its bark unblemished along a thirty-foot trunk—trembles before the assault. Its roots break up through the soil in a taut yet delicate network of snapping strands. For a second or two the uprooted tree appears poised like a startled animal; then it crashes, splintering as it falls, flailing downward through trees of the same generation, snapping off their branches with a crackle that sounds like gunfire.

The D-9 bulldozer is the largest built by the Caterpillar Tractor Corporation. It weighs some forty-eight tons and is priced at $108,000. With a blade that weighs five thousand pounds, rising five feet and curved like some monstrous scimitar, it shears away not only soil and trees but a thousand other things—grapevines, briars, ferns, toadstools, wild garlic, plantain, dandelions, moss, a colony of pink ladyslippers, fragmented slate, an ancient plow point, a nest of squeaking field mice—and sends them hurtling down the slope, an avalanche of the organic and the inorganic, the living and the dead. The larger trees that stand in the path of the bulldozer—persimmons, walnuts, mulberries, oaks, and butternuts—meet the same fate. Toppled, they are crushed and buried in the tide of rubble.

As the days pass, the immense gaping wound crawls ever farther along the ridge, and the flat or "bench" continues to widen. Eventually—as on parts of Big Black Mountain—the sheer, man-made cliff or "highwall" may tower in a raw escarpment of rock, soil, and slate to a height of ninety feet, and the cut into the hill may open an expanse as much as seventy-five feet wide. In the wake of the advancing bulldozers, explosions will be detonated to loosen the coal; then power shovels will lift it into huge Mack trucks, whose twenty-five-ton loads will cause the mountain to tremble once again as they move off with a roar.

The mountain does not yield easily to the machines; its treasure is encased in a ledge of tough sandstone that must be blasted away. The explosives pile the shattered cap rock in towering heaps of spoil along the outer edge of the cut, or send it thundering down the dead flank of the hill. Whole communities tremble as the strings of explosive charges are set off in a process known to the industry as "casting the overburden."

As the stripping continues at one level after another, the entire forest cover vanishes into the rubble. Here and there, miraculously, a little island of green may escape the plunging boulders and the cascades of sliding soil. Where they linger, the trees lean precipitously, perhaps to be finally dislodged by a landslide that catapults them, still upright, onto the valley floor.

Sometimes—though not always—the shovels are followed by augers that drill into the sheer face of the seam, pulling out the shattered coal by the same action as a brace and bit that sends shavings flying as it bores into a plank. These drilling machines are priced at more than $150,000; the exact figure is determined by the size of the bit, which may be as much as six feet in diameter and may be extended, section by section, to a depth of 170 feet. Diesel powered, they are a match for bulldozers and dynamite in sheer violence as well as noise—a shrieking reverberation that deafens while it tumbles out a gush of black fragments that can fill a truck in a minute or less. For an auger of the largest gauge, working an eight-hour shift without interruption, the output can be prodigious—as much as one thousand, five hundred tons per man employed in the operation.

Sometimes contour stripping is used simply to get at the outcrop, the narrow outer remnant of a coal vein that cannot be reached by conventional underground procedures. For this greedy operation the surface of an entire hillside may be dismantled. On the other hand, the coal veins in a hill may be "virgin"—which is to say that no mining has ever taken place there. When the coal is "faced up" and augered, less than 20 percent of the total content can be obtained. The rest is generally beyond the deepest penetration of the huge bit. Deep mining, if it is to be practiced later on, can take place only where a solid wall of undisturbed coal from twenty-five to fifty feet wide has been left as a barrier around the auger holes. The need for stability in the roof of the mine and for the conservation of air make this necessary. As a result, the working area is so restricted that tunneling is usually dismissed as unprofitable. Thus a sizable deposit of coal is lost unless there is a later decision simply to blast away the mountain, layer after layer, from the top downward. When this is done, the rubble that gathers on the valley floor creeps upward as the mountain is sliced away, until the entire range is obliterated. In its place is a wasteland of displaced soil, slabs of rock and slate, and shattered residues of coal and sulfur. All that is left of what was once a tree-covered, living ridge is a vast mesa where nothing moves except the clouds of dust on dry, windy days, or the sluicing autumn rains that carve new creekbeds across its dead surface. It has become an Appalachian Carthage, the beginning of a New World Sahara.

The impact of rain on strip-mined land is immediate and catastrophic. Without leaves or branches to impede its fall, each drop strikes like a whiplash. Enormous gullies are cut into the slopes, and sheets of soil are carried away from more nearly level surfaces. Streams that had run clear for thousands of years are now mud, "too thin to plow and too thick to drink." The rate at which creek- and riverbeds gather silt in the strip-mined region of McCreary County, Kentucky, has been studied by a number of state and federal agencies, and the results have been published by the U.S. Department of the Interior. In two valleys encompassing virtually the same land area, silt traps were installed to measure the comparative accumulation. For Helton Branch, draining an area that had not been strip-mined, the accumulation of silt amounted to 27.9 tons per square mile. For Cane Branch, in an area that had been "effected" or "disturbed"—to use euphemisms dear to the industry—by surface mining, the accumulation per square mile was no less than 30,000 tons!

Eventually, in compliance with the plan for so-called reclamation on file at the state capital, the seeds of fescue and lespedeza will be strewn over the wrecked surface. If the mining operator is really "concerned," he may plant a few hundred pine seedlings to each acre. Patches of spindly grass will take root, and some stunted pines will go on struggling to survive among the gullied spoil heaps. This done, the bonds will be duly released, and the land officially described as having been "reclaimed." And, while the cocktail-party discussion of how our environment is deteriorating goes on and on, the mess that has been left will likewise continue to be ignored.

In Appalachia, streams that have been killed by industry and that are patently useless for any other purpose are being turned into open dumps. The abundant rainfall of the region travels seaward and into the nation's reservoirs through a jumble of privy wastes, rusting tin cans, discarded mattresses, abandoned cars, dead animals, bottles, cardboard boxes, broken toys, rotting table garbage such as was once used to fatten hogs, dishwater, soapsuds, animal manure, and unnameable varieties of filth. In the heartland of a region where the Shenandoah, the Rappahannock, the James, the Roanoke—streams whose very names are intertwined with the nation's heritage—have their rise, pollution holds sway. And every day that pollution widens, hastened by bulldozers—a spreading cancer that may one day engulf a continent.

CHAPTER VII

Coal is our universal companion. Through its by-products, this grimy fuel finds its way into an astonishing assortment of products more or less indispensable to a civilized existence—including synthetic fibers, paints, dyes, medicines, explosives, plastics, fertilizers, insecticides, refrigerants, and photographic sensitizers, along with its more obvious uses, including blacktop roads. Coal is an ingredient of pneumatic tires, and of pain-killers such as aspirin and Demerol. In fact, according to the U.S. Department of the Interior, the single most valuable mineral deposit on earth is not the oilfields of Arabia, not the South African diamond beds, but the coal of Appalachia, stretching from western Pennsylvania southward through the Virginias into Alabama.

Because this black treasure has never come easily from the land, the suffering of the miners who extract it from underground has long been proverbial. In nineteenth-century England they were nothing less than serfs. In those man-made caverns, lit by the flicker of candles or whale-oil lamps, where the lack of ventilation made the heat and humidity all but intolerable, half-naked women and children were hired to push the creaking coal cars along the tunnels or to drag loads of the mineral up ladders in a human conveyor belt. Many died of heart failure on those ladders, to be buried alongside husbands or brothers who had perished in cave-ins or explosions. The rights of these pitiable creatures under the law were as negligible as their earnings. Until 1799 a Scottish miner could not leave that employment without the consent of his master. Before 1815, the death of a "mere collier" was not subject to a coroner's inquest. Compensation for disability and death came slowly and grudgingly. Strikes, slowdowns, or any form of trade unionism were prohibited as inimical to "sound public policy," or even downright treasonous. The cost in human suffering of extracting the fuel without which the industrial revolution, and the predominance of Britain as a commercial power, would have been impossible is a cost that cannot be measured and can scarcely even be imagined.

And when in America the reliance on charcoal ended and mining in Maryland and Pennsylvania began, the methods were no less pernicious, the attitudes no less callous, than in the Old World. In fact, many of the pits were opened by mine masters from Scotland and Wales. Countless freeborn natives and freedom-seeking immigrants became slaves to the molelike routine of working in the mines. They lived, as generations after them were to do, in remote settlements along canals and railroads, where a growing nation took little heed of them. With their warped limbs and soot-blackened lungs they died as they had lived, in obscurity.

Even now, despite continued proclamations by political and industrial spokesmen of the superiority of the United States in every field, the treatment of the nation's subterranean coal miners and their families remains literally obscene. While the Congress has been lavish with tariffs, import quotas, subsidies, and bonuses to shore up the producers of wheat, cotton, and tobacco, the airlines, the building and banking industries, among many others, in our system of alleged free enterprise the employees of the coal industry have become the victims of an operation that, in practice as well as theory, is indeed at the mercy of the marketplace.

Even during the vast industrial expansion that was fostered by World War II, coal was left to develop as it might, while tank and bomber factories, among countless new enterprises, were underwritten by the U.S. treasury. To meet the needs of the global conflict, the coal industry carried on the well-tried practice of enticing boys and youths away from school and into the mines. Those boys are in and around the mines today—most of them sick and broken hulks, worn out by their early forties. While in Western Europe a series of social and industrial reforms have steadily reduced the human attrition of the coal mines, in our own country there has been much in pious declarations of legislative intent, but little in the way of tightly enforced safety procedures. A comparison of the fatality records tells the story. In the years following the end of World War II, the death rates per hundred thousand underground man shifts ranged, in Great Britain, from a high of 0.44 in 1944 to a low of 0.24 in 1954; in Belgium, from 0.66 in 1953 to 0.32 in 1955; in West Germany, from 0.77 in 1948 to 0.61 in 1955. During the same period in the United States, the fatality rate dropped from 1.22 in 1947 to a mere 0.84 in 1952—and rose again to 1.07 in 1963.

That the business of bringing up coal from underground shafts is a dangerous one at present cannot be denied. That it must continue to be so is highly arguable. Little effort has been made to date to bring the benefits of modern medicine, either curative or preventive, to the working face. Enormous outlays of both capital and ingenuity have been expended on the technology of the operation. For example, a twenty-ton, self-propelled mining machine is capable of hurling ten tons of coal a minute onto a conveyor belt. A tube of compressed air can exert twenty thousand pounds of pressure to the square inch inside a vein, loosening huge quantities within seconds. Continuous longwall-mining devices can recover coal at a rate exceeding 220 tons a day. A coal plow that operates like a planing tool along a solid face is capable of bringing up coal faster than it can be carried away. These and many other innovations have steadily increased the rate of production, at the same time that they have reduced working payrolls from a peak of 704,793 men in 1923 to approximately 131,000 in 1969. But the hazards faced by the men who accompany the machines have been little diminished. In 1963, a total of 284 men were killed and 11,090 others were disabled. In 1969, at least 203 perished.

In November 1968, an explosion roared through a large mine, Mountaineer No. 9, operated by Consolidation Coal Company at Mannington, West Virginia. The anguished faces of women and children keeping vigil near the shaft went out over television screens throughout the country, bringing a momentary surge of public dismay and horror. In response, the president of the United Mine Workers, W. A. (Tony) Boyle, was quoted as saying, "I know what it's like to be in an explosion. I've gone through several of them"—adding that there was always "this inherent danger connected with mining coal," and that Consol was "one of the better companies to work with." A little later, there was an admission from the U.S. Bureau of Mines that although Mountaineer No. 9 had been repeatedly found in violation of federal safety regulations then in effect, no action had been taken against the company. "Close a Consol mine? You must be kidding," T. N. Bethell reports an official of the Bureau as having said in reply to a question. "Any inspector who closed a Consol mine would be looking for another job the next day."

There was, however, enough uneasiness over the fate of the miners to evoke something like a call for action. Secretary of the Interior Stewart Udall—who, as Ben Franklin of the *Times* observed, for eight years had displayed "more concern for California Redwoods than for miners"—declared that "we have accepted, even condoned, an attitude of fatalism that belongs to an age darker than the deepest recesses of any coal mine." And his successor, Walter J. Hickel, ventured a statement that was, surprisingly, even stronger: "It is clear that our society can no longer tolerate the cost in human life and human misery that is exacted in the mining of this essential fuel. Unless we find ways to eliminate this intolerable cost, we must inevitably limit our mining of coal . . ."

But there was still no senator from a coal state eager to challenge the combined might of the coal, steel, railroad, and electrical power cabal and its political war chests. Thus the task of steering a tough federal mine safety bill through the Senate fell to Harrison Williams, Jr., of New Jersey—a state with no coal deposits. Even though the Nixon Administration had called for such a bill, its provisions could easily have gone the way of previous futile attempts on behalf of mining safety. As a member of the Labor subcommittee headed by Senator Williams, Senator Jennings Randolph of West Virginia offered a set of proposals of his own—which Ralph Nader, the consumer advocate and general gadfly, declared in a letter to Randolph to have been inspired by the coal industry. In reply, John Corcoran, president of Consolidation Coal Company and chairman of the National Coal Association, admitted that a number of the provisions in the Randolph bill had been "suggested" by him and other executives in the coal industry, but insisted that it was only natural for him to discuss such matters with the senator since they had been "good friends" for years. Other efforts to weaken the bill came from Senator John Sherman Cooper of Kentucky, with the backing of another Republican, Senator Howard Baker of Tennessee.

In the House, a similar bill was sponsored by Representative John H. Dent, a Pennsylvania Democrat. The most determined of its long list of cosponsors, Representative Ken Hechler of West Virginia, earned a denunciation from Tony Boyle for suggesting that the union had done less than it might on behalf of miners suffering from black lung. It was Hechler who put pressure on the White House to force an evidently reluctant Bureau of Mines into releasing the results of a study indicating that the dust level in coal mines could be reduced by the use of high-pressure ventilation equipment at the working face. In the same way, Ralph Nader—whom Boyle also angrily denounced for his statements about the UMW and the coal industry—accused the Interior Department of suppressing a report on the environmental effects of underground mining, so as not to expose the industry to public criticism while the mine safety bill was being debated by the House subcommittee. A week after the subcommittee approved the bill, the study was made available for public inspection. On October 2, 1969, the Senate approved the Williams bill by a vote of 73–0; on October 29, by a vote of 389–4, the House approved its version. Both bills were considerably more stringent than the six-point proposal originally offered by the Administration—and clearly much stronger than President Nixon really wanted. The opposition, led in the House by one William J. Scherle, a Republican from Iowa, moved to recommit the bill with instructions to delete the grant of compensation to miners with black lung. The move failed, even though Secretary of Labor George P. Schultz invoked the prerogative of the states to deal with workmen's compensation, adding that he also thought it would cost too much. Word went out that the President might veto the bill for that very reason—an announcement that *The New York Times* called "inexcusable" in both timing and intent. On December 17, 1969, the House voted 333–12 for the bill, which had emerged virtually unaltered from a Senate-House conference. It was not until December 29, during a visit to the White House by the widows of the seventy-eight miners killed in the blast at Farmington, West Virginia—arranged by Representative Hechler—that the President's decision to sign the bill was announced. The next day it became law as the National Coal Mine Safety Act of 1969. As of 1971, its stringent regulations were yet to be enforced.[1]

[1] On May 31, 1971, the General Accounting Office issued an eighty-page report charging that the record of the Bureau of Mines in enforcing the Federal Mine Safety Act was "extremely lenient, confusing, uncertain and inequitable." According to a report by Ben Franklin in *The New York Times* for June 1, 1971, "The G.A.O. report said that in the two major areas that it had checked in the Appalachian coal fields, only 31 per cent of the number of mine safety inspections required by the act and only 1 per cent of the required health inspections were made by the bureau in 1970. At the same time, the Bureau of Mines itself reported that the death toll in 1970 had

One reason was the presence in the Department of the Interior of Fred J. Russell, a California real estate millionaire, who as undersecretary was in charge of the department from the departure of Secretary Hickel in November 1970 until the appointment of Rogers C. B. Morton as Secretary of the Interior in February of the following year. Months before Hickel resigned, however, Russell—whom Representative Hechler described as "a true troglodyte of the McKinley era"—had given orders to the Bureau of Mines that before exercising the power to close a mine found to be in violation of the new mine safety act, safety inspectors were to ask for telephoned authorization from Washington. Then, in February, shortly after Morton took office, Russell got around to announcing the makeup of a technical advisory committee on coal mine safety research. Under the law, the committee was to have been appointed and functioning a year earlier. Of its thirteen members, seven turned out to have no technical qualifications—one was a former airline stewardess—but all were discovered to have proved their loyalty as members of the Republican party. The disclosure was embarrassing enough to the new secretary that a week later Russell lost his job.

Even for those less dedicated to the cause of the mining interests, action on behalf of their victims is not easy. In early 1968, when Senator Robert Kennedy tried to inspect a strip mine in eastern Kentucky, he found his way blocked by a company foreman. The power of the coal companies was long ago and forcibly demonstrated in Kentucky, when Alben Barkley ran for governor, and dared to call for a tax on coal. It was the only election that redoubtable politician ever lost. That was in 1923, and nearly fifty years afterward no candidate for the governorship had yet gone so far in challenging the industry.

Perhaps the day was coming for Kentucky, as it had for West

'worsened appreciably,' with a total of 260, or 57 more than in 1969. And Senator Harrison Williams raised the possibility of transferring the responsibility of enforcing the mine safety law from the Interior Department to the Labor Department."

Virginia—a state fortunate enough to have been adopted by two remarkable men whom the voters had the good sense to elect to public office. One was Congressman Ken Hechler, a former New Yorker and onetime college professor. On February 18, 1971, he dropped into the legislative hopper a bill bearing the names of twenty-nine cosponsors and designed to outlaw strip mining for coal totally throughout the United States. Meanwhile, West Virginia's Secretary of State, John D. Rockefeller IV—"Jay" to his adopted compatriots—had endorsed a bill introduced by State Senator Si Galperin to outlaw strip mining in West Virginia "completely and forever," and had set off a political earthquake in the process.

Rockefeller called a press conference late in 1970 to denounce the state's strip-mine law, passed in 1967, as unenforceable. Why? Because there are Fred Russells in every government, including West Virginia's. The State Director of Natural Resources in 1970 confessed that he hadn't refused a single application from a strip miner seeking a permit under the 1967 law. In 1970 the area subjected to stripping rose 109 percent over the previous year. Five counties have been totally stripped of their coal deposits; the process in 1971 was going on in twenty-eight others and was the dismal prospect for ten more out of the fifty-five counties that make up the nation's largest producer of coal. A deputy director of Natural Resources, Norman Williams, braved the wrath of the strippers to plead: "The people who are making the decisions about strip-mining aren't the people who have to live with the consequences. If they were, strip-mining would be outlawed tomorrow."[2] It wasn't, of course. Instead, Senator Galperin, who had drafted the bill Rockefeller endorsed, was dropped from the special subcommittee that had been appointed to consider it, and a travesty was enacted in its place.

Rockefeller came to West Virginia as a VISTA worker and stayed on to serve a term in the state legislature before being

[2] Quoted in *Coal Patrol*, published by Appalachia Information, Washington, D.C., March 1, 1971.

elected Secretary of State. Unless his latest undertaking brings him to grief, this scion of New York's wealthiest family is likely to be elected governor in 1972. It is of course possible that both he and Congressman Hechler may be defeated, as Alben Barkley was—or even finally driven from public life—by sustained, lavishly financed campaigns. In any event, their efforts suggest a measure of the despair that grips intelligent people when they contemplate the destruction visited on the land they inhabit.

CHAPTER VIII

In 1964 the Congress of the United States passed the Appalachian Regional Development Act. Since then, over a billion dollars have been appropriated and poured into a jurisdiction covering parts of thirteen states. Most of the money has gone into road building—as is hardly surprising, since roads are beloved of corporations engaged in extractive activities, and since in mountain regions a cut less than a mile long may cost millions of dollars. In June 1970, Ben Franklin reported in a dispatch to *The New York Times:*

Five years and several billion dollars later, the Government officials who manage the Appalachian economic recovery effort initiated by President Kennedy have decided the time has come to "reach the people." . . . On a tour by chartered bus over 750 miles of mountain road in six states, the officials acknowledged that the money spent here since the first massive Appalachian funding in 1965 has had little or no direct impact on the hill people whose plight had moved President Kennedy to start the program in the first place.

On the subject of the Appalachian Regional Commission, whose responsibility it is to improve the lot of the poor hill people, an environmental newsletter is even more heavily ironic: the commission, it notes, "is doing its part to 'protect the environment' by giving Kentucky a $550,000 grant to 'study' strip-mining over the next three years in an effort to decide what, if anything, to do about it." [1] Yet evidently the touring officials meant well, at least while they were on the spot; before they headed back for Washington, to disappear into the air-conditioned corridors of the bureaucracy, Ben Franklin reported that they "were calling for a severance or extraction tax on coal to make the industry pay for its depredations. . . . 'It's like taxing the churches in Rome, I guess,' one official on the tour commented, 'but we are probably coming to something like that.'" Like St. Augustine crying "Save me, Lord—but not yet," the intent may have been real, though actually reaching the people is another matter.

In fact, regional development in an area like Appalachia, rich in resources but impoverished by exploitation, becomes virtually impossible when the real masters of the region are the corporations that own and deal in these resources. The unchecked power of the corporations is, of course, a matter of concern not for Appalachia alone. As an editorial in the *Manchester Guardian Weekly* for March 7, 1970, noted, "Some already see the day—not too far off—when the giant international corporations will be answerable to no national government. The new international industrial groups threaten to grow more powerful than any one nation state." The same observer might have gone on to note that the American states have failed consistently and ignominiously in their occasional efforts to curb the sprawling enterprises that extract, manufacture, and sell with mindless disregard for every consideration except that of corporate profit. It might further have been asserted that the federal government is hardly less ineffectual in dealing with conglomerate entities such as A.T.&T. or Standard Oil of New Jersey. We live, in short, in a society where a telephone call from the president of a steel corporation carries

[1] *Coal Patrol*, published by Appalachia Information, Washington, D.C., March 1, 1971.

more influence with those in office than a petition signed by tens of thousands of ordinary, one-vote citizens.

And what of the economic baronies that have hauled away such immense, virtually untaxed fortunes in coal, oil, natural gas, limestone, and timber from the hills of Appalachia? Few people have any clear idea of who owns them or of what their operations consist. In general, the companies that have gone about extracting the mineral wealth of the region are not only obscure but also small by any absolute standard. Few Kentuckians, for example, could explain the nature of the Virginia Coal and Iron Company, more recently known as the Penn-Virginia Company, which acquired the mineral rights on some two hundred thousand acres of land in western Virginia, eastern Kentucky, and West Virginia during the 1880s and 1890s. At about the same time, other corporations were turning vast stretches of Latin America into colonial fiefdoms; and just as order has been maintained among the Latin peoples by the U.S. Marines, in eastern Kentucky the preserve of Penn-Virginia and others like it has been maintained by sheriffs, state policemen, company-hired gunmen, the state militia, and the National Guard. Rarely has so much as a glimpse been afforded behind the curtain of anonymity that cloaks such entities; but now and then it does happen, as when Thomas Murphy, a reporter for *Dun's Review and Modern Industry*, was granted an interview with Edward Leisenring, president of what was then the Virginia Coal and Iron Company.

Here is Mr. Murphy's account of an eastern Kentucky landlord:

America's Most Profitable Company?

From plain, green-painted offices in Philadelphia's South Broad Street, tall, tweedy Edward B. Leisenring, Jr. runs what may well be the most profitable company in all of American industry. Certainly few other companies can come close to the 61% margin that Leisenring's Virginia Coal & Iron Co. shows on its revenues. By way of comparison, mighty General Motors brings 10.2% of its sales dollars down to net, AT&T 15.5% and U. S. Steel 5.7%.

Though it has large holdings of railroad stocks, Virginia Coal & Iron obtains 54% of its income from coal royalties . . . and stumpage (the highly profitable, depletion-blessed trees that grow in the soil over its diggings). All told, Virginia Coal leases out 10,000 acres of land in West Virginia, 100,000 acres in Kentucky and southwestern Virginia and 5,000 acres in western Pennsylvania. In West Virginia alone, its lands are estimated to hold 116.9 million tons of coal.

Leisenring carries nearly all the income from these activities right down to net. During 1964, for example, royalties, dividends and rental on a coke plant gave Virginia Coal & Iron a total income of $2.5 million. From that came expenses of $745,875, hardly enough to pay the salaries of three steel executives. Thanks to depletion and capital gains, taxes took out $221,139—leaving net earnings of $1.5 million, or 61% of Virginia Coal & Iron's total income.

Even that, though, does not accurately sum up the wealth that was accumulated for the company's shareholders. Earnings were further bolstered by a gain on the sale of coal in place of $101,538. So earnings, all told, came to $1.6 million, or $3.45 a share, up from $1.3 million, or $2.81 a share, for 1963.

There is, of course, no secret to the source of Virginia Coal's wealth. As a lessor of land to coal mining companies, the company has few expenses of its own. "Only real-estate taxes, really," says Howard H. Frey, assistant to the president. "We do have occasions when we're proving additional coal, and we test a land's deposits by boring or core drilling to about 150 feet."

But that is really the only large expense. The mining company does the rest. "You depend on the honorableness of your lessee," says Frey, "so you've got to deal with people you can trust." He adds: "In a case where the lessee leaves more coal than he could have recovered, we charge him on an estimated basis."

Logging the company's woodlands also involves little labor or expense on the part of Virginia Coal. For this, too, is done by outside contractors. In Virginia, for example, the Hamer Lumber Corp. cruises its properties and takes off the hardwood for a minimum royalty of $60,000 a year. With perpetual care now the vogue in forestry, moreover, Virginia can count on getting its hardwoods harvested again in forty years, no great amount of time in terms of corporate history.

Lessees also work Virginia Coal's properties for gas, an unheard-of commodity years ago when some of the lands were sold to the company for pennies an acre. Where gas is present, it is true, the coal-miner must leave a certain amount of coal in the ground as a casing. But since gas comes under roughly the same tax laws as coal, but with even more favorable economics, this is no hardship at all.

As if all that were not enough, there also is the matter of Virginia's bulging stock portfolio. Obtained largely by the sale of its own railroad that once ran across its lands, it now holds no less than 275,000 shares of common stock in the Southern Railway, probably one of the best-managed rails in all the land. These holdings pay Virginia about $770,000 in dividends a year. Yet even that is hardly calculated to add to the company's tax burden, for under the Internal Revenue laws, 85% of the dividends paid by one corporation to another are tax-free.

And, of course, in none of its lines does Virginia Coal & Iron come anywhere near to what might be called a businessman's risk. For all the company's mining, and all the chance-taking, is done by other companies who hope to find oil, gas or coal (there is also some limestone and some sandstone) on the Virginia Coal & Iron lands. "When you lease," says Howard Frey, "the operator takes the risk of putting up a cleaning plant and tippler, and we take the depletion deduction. It's the widows and orphans versus the prospectors."

And for the prudent, tax-wise Philadelphians who run Virginia Coal & Iron, events have proven that it is always better to be on the side of the widows and orphans.

That was in April 1965. As of September 1966, this extraordinary firm had nineteen employees. More recently it has acquired 18 percent of the stock of Can-Fer, Ltd., a base-metal exploration company in Toronto. Its roster of stockholders reads like a

"Who's Who in New York and Philadelphia." The annual property taxes paid by its huge landholdings average about forty-five cents an acre. The process at work here has been explained by Ferdinand Lundberg in his massively documented study of American economic power, *The Rich and the Super-Rich:*

What all the expansion reflects is: investment of earnings not paid out. . . . Payouts incur additional taxes for stockholders; retained invested earnings are not taxed, are like money in the bank and get accelerated depreciation allowances. . . . Let us take a . . . sober-seeming company, the Mississippi River Fuel Corporation, originally formed to transport natural gas by pipeline from Louisiana to St. Louis. There was first formed the Mississippi River Corporation to exchange stock with it, and this company now owns 94.2 per cent of the Mississippi Transmission Corporation, 100 per cent of several cement companies and 58 per cent of the Class A stock of the big Missouri Pacific Railroad. As the change in its name suggests, it is apparently going to concern itself with everything in the Mississippi Valley, perhaps the Valley as a whole. . . . The time, then, is near at hand when a company's name will give no clue at all to its line of business apart from the business of making money.

Exactly as with Penn-Virginia. The landowning companies, their mining, drilling, and lumbering lessees, the railroads, barge lines, and transmission pipeline companies and the coal-burning electric utilities make up a phalanx of interlocking interests and powers that dominate the political life of every state any part of which falls within the Appalachian coalfields. Of all these captives, Kentucky is probably the most debased and servile.

Of the firms with huge colonial holdings in the Kentucky mountains, the Kentucky River Coal Corporation is almost the equal of Penn-Virginia in obscurity, and perhaps in profits. There are others such as the Big Sandy Corporation, with headquarters in Campobello, Maine; Elkhorn Coal Corporation; Virginia Iron, Coal and Coke Company; Fordson Coal and Timber Company, a subsidiary of Ford Motor Company; and still others whose names are, for one reason or another, relatively familiar—U.S. Steel, Republic Steel, Bethlehem Steel, Occidental Petroleum, and Consolidation Coal. And among these giants, the trading goes on even in Kentucky.

For example, in 1956 Consolidation Coal Company, at a price reported to have been sixteen million dollars, sold its mining interests in the Kentucky hills to a subsidiary of Bethlehem Steel Corporation. For tax purposes, the property was assessed at less than 10 percent of the reported selling price—a statistic that once again helps to explain the grinding poverty of the region.

Although the area had been heavily mined in some places, at least half was undisturbed. Some of the veins were more than twelve feet thick, and nearly all of them consisted of an extremely hard coal eminently suited for metallurgical use. Bethlehem's investment in Pike County produced what is probably the most highly mechanized coal mining operation in the world. Between 1956 and 1969, the nation's second largest producer of steel ran ahead of its huge competitor U.S. Steel in technological innovation and profits to its stockholders. Besides extracting millions of tons of coal for its furnaces, Bethlehem also leased sections of the same region for limestone, oil, and gas operations. In its treatment of the Appalachian land and people the corporation displayed a relatively benign and enlightened attitude. It sealed scores of old mine portals, stanching the flow of acid-contaminated underground waters into creeks and rivers. Local spokesmen asserted that the corporation viewed its thousands of forested acres as a resource highly valuable in itself, and much too beautiful to ruin with strip mining. For a couple of years, indeed, all stripping was halted, and at gatherings of conservationists across the state Bethlehem received high marks. Compared with the record of Consolidation Coal, it appeared a paragon of corporate restraint. But as things turned out, the congratulations were somewhat premature.

According to Ferdinand Lundberg, the largest, and probably the controlling, interest in Bethlehem is held by the Mellon family, whose fortune amounts to some six billion dollars. *The New York Times* for June 6, 1969, carried an account by Sarah Booth Conroy of an interview with Mrs. Paul Mellon at her estate near Upperville in the hunt country of Virginia. After being admitted by guards in a red wooden house at the entrance to the grounds, the reporter had driven along a winding, tree-shaded road to the U-shaped, two-story country residence where the Mellons were then at home. A mile or so away stood another, larger mansion that had been converted to house a collection of works of art. Mrs. Mellon said that her other residences were in New York, in Washington, D.C., in Osterville, Massachusetts, and at Antigua in the West Indies.

After a stroll through an entrance foyer lined with geranium trees, Mrs. Mellon led her guest to the library, where they lunched on "tiny, tiny asparagus with butter and lemon," cottage cheese, and a salad flavored with fresh herbs. The food had all been produced on the estate, the reporter was told, except for the brown sugar that was passed with the coffee. That had been imported from England. On a tour of the grounds, past the swimming pool and tennis court, the gardens and conservatory, Mrs. Mellon wore a poppy-red hat from Balenciaga. "I've always been dressed by him," she said. "I like the way his clothes move."

According to the reporter, the Paul Mellons are considered the leading art collectors in the world. All told, the Mellon family, acting individually or through foundations, has given away an estimated $700 million over the last two generations. But the monumental triviality of the interview on that June day is of interest principally because of what was being said at almost precisely the same time by the superintendent of Bethlehem Steel's operations in eastern Kentucky, one David A. Zegeer. At a press conference in his office in the mining town of Jenkins, he announced that the company believed it could actually improve the land by stripping it!

Outlining the company's plans, Zegeer said they would include clear-cutting of all the second-growth timber on the property. He could not estimate the quantity of oak, poplar, beech, maple, tulip poplar, and other varieties of wood to be removed and marketed, but conceded that it "will be substantial, of course." Thus some seven million tons of coal for Bethlehem's mills and furnaces would become accessible. Three seams would be mined; in order to avoid a "public image problem," the land would then be quickly restored. Color slides of blackberry bushes growing on old spoil banks were displayed, and there was talk of transforming other such disfigurements into "mountain meadows," where cows, their udders sagging with milk, would graze on ryegrass, timothy, and clover.

For all the glossy forecast of the public relations brochures, conservationists were appalled. No one acquainted with the steep slopes and heavy rainfall of mountain Kentucky was inclined to accept such a prospect. Pleas from a variety of organizations poured in, urging Bethlehem's directors to revert to their earlier policy of no strip mining. Among them was a letter from Elvis Stahr, formerly Secretary of the Army and now president of the National Audubon Society, to S. S. Cort, president of Bethlehem Steel, dated September 22, 1969. Pointing out that most of the remaining coal could be mined by efficient subterranean methods having a minimum impact on the surface and its ecology, the letter declared: "Conservationists everywhere deplore the prospect that your corporation may destroy this beautiful land, with its superb stands of second-growth hardwoods, for this tiny remnant of coal. If stripping occurs as planned, the last vestiges of minerals will have been wrung from the earth but the land itself will have been wrecked." Mindful of the care and the large sums that corporate managers can expend on cultivating an appearance of concern for the environment, Mr. Stahr ended the letter by saying, "We believe that if your lands are preserved the harvest of good will more than offset any temporary economic loss the company may sustain."

It was soon clear, however, that Bethlehem Steel was not really seeking any harvest of good will. "Enlightened leadership in preserving the Appalachian land" was not, after all, their forte; what concerned them was a harvest of profits from the quick sale of wood and coal. Thus, the letters of protest and entreaty from spokesmen for the World Wildlife Fund, the Izaak Walton League of America, the Kentucky Conservation Council, and the Kentucky Chapter of the Sierra Club, among many others, simply went ignored. The bulldozers went into action, and a torrent of coal gushed from within the mangled slopes.

The first operation was undertaken by Bethlehem's lessee, Tackett and Manning Trucking Company, on Millstone Creek in Letcher County. Despite a proclaimed intention of "exceeding the requirements" of the Kentucky reclamation law, the work was begun with insouciant disregard for either the law or public concern. On October 28, 1969, a notice of noncompliance was sent to the operator by the state's Director of Reclamation. On November 11, all work was suspended by an order that listed at least four violations. A week later, the suspension order was quietly lifted, and the "development" went forward once more. As delegations of students and environmentalists began arriving to stare in horror at the stripped hills, Bethlehem shifted its operations to Beefhide Creek, which was remote and difficult to reach.

In the spring of 1970, the devastated slopes of Millstone Valley were hydro-seeded with timothy, ryegrass, lespedeza, and fescue. Here and there, some pines were set out. Patches of grass, urged on by a heavy application of chemical fertilizer, emerged among the slabs of slate and alongside silt-choked streams. Within a matter of weeks, as the effect of the fertilizer was exhausted, the bright green of the grass had faded to the pale and sickly tint that presages failure. Meanwhile, the reclamation bonds have been discharged, and the land officially certified as "reclaimed." And the spokesmen for Bethlehem Steel were still at work. "Sure, mining disturbs the earth," said David Zegeer. "But we're conserving a natural resource by extracting a needed fuel that would otherwise be wasted."

The contrast between the ruin spread across the slopes of Millstone Valley and the lush, carefully tended acres at Upperville are perhaps a portent for the future: a few oases of beauty and ease for the very rich; for the rest of mankind, desolation and squalor. How far the industries and their spokesmen are from any concern with such a prospect was indicated by a full-page advertisement in *The Voice*, published at Hazard, Kentucky, in the heart of the coal country, on February 19, 1970. Over the names of the Deleware Power Company and a list of its dealers, critics of strip mining were described as "high-minded heroes" who "decry the rape of natural resources and bemoan polluted streams and air." But strip mining, the advertisement continued, "is not a political or social issue. It is economical. It has to do with dollars."

In Millstone Valley, a lawsuit against Bethlehem Steel, asking $2.1 million in damages for "wanton, reckless disregard" of the rights of property owners was filed in 1969, with Luther M. Johnson as plaintiff. As a result, he was soon receiving threats from the strip-mine operators. "They are just going to ruin all the land here for the dollar if we don't stop them," Mr. Johnson said, and added, "Now I like a dollar as well as anyone. But this land would go on forever if they wouldn't wreck it. And against that, money doesn't seem of much account."

CHAPTER IX

In a sense, strip mining may be almost as old as the human race. When a primitive hunter broke a flint shard from a ledge and fashioned it into a spear point, he was already engaging in the simplest form of surface mining. Ages later, having discovered the utility first of copper and then of iron for tools and weapons, he began digging to unearth in larger quantities the ores he had first taken from outcroppings. Deep mining, the sinking of shafts and the excavation of tunnels, came only in comparatively recent times—probably within the last three or four thousand years. And the large-scale mining of coal is more recent still, if less so than is commonly supposed. Lewis Mumford points out, for example, that mining and smelting were already advanced industries by the sixteenth century, and cites figures given by John U. Nef: [1] "from 1564 to 1634 the recorded shipments of coal from the Tyne increased nearly fourteen times over, from 32,952 tons to 452,625 tons." [2]

Geologists estimate that of approximately 3.6 trillion tons of

[1] *War and Human Progress: An Essay on the Rise of Industrial Civilization* (Cambridge, Mass., 1952).
[2] *The Pentagon of Power* (New York, 1970), p. 146.

coal in deposits across the face of the earth, nearly half—some 1.66 trillion—are buried under American soil. As industrialization proceeds unchecked here and abroad, the appetite for coal likewise increases. Of an annual production that in 1970 stood at about 556 million tons, 56 million tons went overseas. Ten years earlier, the total output had been 419 million tons; by 1974, the National Coal Association expected the demand to have risen to 650 million tons.

While members of Congress have begun asking for a curb on shipments of coal, especially that having a low sulfur content, to Japan, capital from that fast-growing industrial nation is already going into the financing of an enormous complex of new mines. In Japan itself, as in the highly developed countries of Western Europe, coal production is on the decline for the simple reason that mining exacts a price their societies are unwilling to pay. As a matter of deliberate policy, the portals are being sealed up and the miners shifted to other industries. These countries are turning to other fuels so far as possible, and they are also using their ample dollar reserves to buy coal from Appalachia and the Midwestern United States. Thus they enjoy the benefits of cheap coal while our own nation pays the penalty of human and economic waste, along with a growing toll of polluted waterways, uprooted woodlands, and ravaged soil.

As the demand for coal goes up, the proportion obtained by stripping also rises. In the ten years from 1960 to 1970, the percentage rose from 29 to 35 percent of the total production in the United States, and within a few years it is expected to rise to half the nation's entire output. The reasons, as outlined by Ben Franklin in *The New York Times* for December 15, 1970, are "the huge demand for cheap steam coal to generate electric power, the costly new requirements of tighter Federal safety regulations in underground mines, and the willingness of coal companies to brave mounting environmental criticism while sales and profits are at record highs . . ."

With the market for strip-mined coal expected to reach a peak within four or five years, and then to decline as stricter environmental regulations ban the use of coal with a high sulfur content, such as is produced by most stripping operations, the rush was on to lap up the gravy. Again according to Ben Franklin:

In Virginia, West Virginia, Kentucky and Tennessee, nearly half the strip mine permits now in force were issued in the last seven months. Many persons rushing into the strip mine business are highway contractors, and others with stocks of heavy machinery but no mining experience. . . . Some spot sales of coal are bringing $8 to $12 a ton, more than the $4 a ton average of the biggest coal producers. . . .

New power stations near sources of coal supplies may bring the strip mining boom to states like North Dakota, Montana and Wyoming, which have large reserves. A report by the U.S. Geological Survey estimated that 26 states have strippable reserves of 128 billion tons, or 690 years' supply at current production rates, and that recovery of it would gouge spoil banks covering 42,000 square miles, an area larger than the state of Ohio.

Senator Harrison Williams observed, as hearings were about to begin on the proposed mine safety bill: "If I read correctly the coal industry's production and fiscal reports, these hearings will not be complicated by the 'bankruptcy' arguments so frequently leveled at this type legislation. The National Coal Association calls its product 'The Fuel of the Future.' In a July 1968 press release, the NCA stated that . . . 'as America's main reservoir of energy in the years ahead, coal's prospects are glittering.' " The senator then went on to cite an article in *Barron's* for July 1968, reporting the acquisition by noncoal companies of the nation's three largest coal producers—Consolidation Coal by Continental Oil in 1966; Island Creek by Occidental Petroleum, and Peabody Coal Company by Kennecott Copper, both in 1968.[3]

[3] According to Ronnie Dugger in "Oil and Politics" (*Atlantic*, September 1969), Continental Oil Company acquired Consolidation Coal under an ABC transaction, a complicated three-party arrangement involving the sale of

In the history of the coal industry, such mergers and acquisitions are nothing new. Consolidation Coal itself is a study in the way they are managed. Here is T. J. Bethell's account:

. . . George Love . . . had moved into the Consolidation Coal Company in 1943. Consol was a shaky giant then, not yet fully recovered from bankruptcy during the Depression. Love proceeded to take control of Consol by merging it with his old company, Union Collieries, and acquiring the majority of the new corporation's stock—a project in which he had the powerful financial help of George Humphrey, then president of the M. A. Hanna Company and later to become President Eisenhower's Secretary of the Treasury and principal guru for domestic affairs.

Once Love and Humphrey had taken control of Consol, they merged it with Pittsburgh Coal Company, and in 1945 Love became president, at the age of 44, of the largest coal company in the United States (Humphrey chose to stay in the background, merely holding 25 per cent—the largest single block—of Consol's stock).

. . . Love thrived in the chaos of the coal industry. In a well-

the mineral interests and the computing of capital gains. "Under IRS rulings," Dugger reported, "the net effect was that the oil company paid no income taxes at all on its $460 million of profits from operating the coal company—profits with which it was buying the company—but *was* permitted to deduct its $128 million in coal-mining costs. The coal company paid no taxes on its income from the sale because it was liquidated under a certain section of the tax code." Senator Albert Gore of Tennessee, who drew attention to the transaction, said he could "foresee a situation, not far off, when we will no longer have an independent coal industry. We may well have all major energy sources—petroleum, coal, uranium—under the control of a very few powerful corporations." Dugger, in the same article, went on to report: "In the last 13 years, 20 oil companies with assets of more than half a billion dollars have acquired 226 other companies and 18,737 gasoline service stations."

Morton Mintz and Jerry S. Cohen, in *America, Inc.* (New York, 1971), noting that by 1970 "Standard Oil of New Jersey had become one of the two largest holders of coal reserves," report that at least eleven of the twenty-five largest oil companies "have significant interests in coal . . . ; and the industry as a whole accounts for at least 25 per cent of coal production."

regulated industry untroubled by overproduction, he might never have built the colossus of Consol. . . . Conditions in the coal industry were allowing him to build an unprecedented economic empire with unprecedented speed . . . In 1961 he took over the Chrysler Corporation when it was on the decline, pouring Consol's money into it and attempting a merger with Mack Trucks, Inc.; the merger was blocked by the Justice Department, thwarting Love for perhaps the first and only time in his career. Through the 1960's, however, he guided Consol's absorption of a number of smaller companies and led the company to constantly higher profits—from $12 million in 1954, for example, to more than $45 million in 1966. . . .

Besides ranking as the largest coal producer in the nation, Consol is also the first company of its importance to have been found guilty by a jury of conspiring with a labor union to take control of an industry. This distinction was conferred by a federal jury at Lexington, Kentucky, just three weeks before the explosion in Consol's Mountaineer No. 9 mine that killed seventy-eight men. According to the verdict, Consol and the United Mine Workers of America had violated the Sherman Anti-trust Act by conspiring since 1950 to function as a monopoly in the production of soft coal. The plaintiff, an operator in eastern Kentucky known as the South-East Coal Company, was awarded $7 million in compensatory damages—half to be paid by the United Mine Workers, the other half by Consol.

Otherwise unimpeded, Consol has proceeded to expand its operations still further. The financial section of *The New York Times* on September 7, 1969, for example, carried an account of a new mine—the property of the Rowland Company, now a division of Consol—at Beckley, West Virginia, where, for what was believed to be the first time, three methods of mining would all be used: continuous mining, electric augers, and surface stripping. John Corcoran, George Love's successor as president of Consol, reported that the mine represented a capital investment of about

$10.5 million, and that it would "go into production late this year and reach capacity in 1970 with 200 employees."

In Belmont County near the eastern border of Ohio, operations in late 1970 were proceeding night and day for Consol's Hanna Division, the owner of some 95,000 acres of what was once rolling farmland—pastures, cornfields, and woodlots dotted with clusters of farm buildings. In one of his best pieces of reporting, Ben Franklin described for readers of *The New York Times* on December 15, 1970, what had been taking place:

Here in Belmont County, whose total area is 346,000 acres, reliable estimates are that 200,000 acres . . . have already been sold, leased or optioned to coal suppliers. Land prices have soared in little over a year, from $150 to $200 an acre to $1,000 to $2,000 and a reported $3,500 an acre. A quarter section here—the house, empty barns and fields of a 150-acre farm—may bring up to $300,000. And there are few holdouts.

. . . The Hanna Division's largest option, in the so-called Egypt Valley field between Cadiz and Barnesville, Ohio, straddles the heavily-traveled, four-lane route of Interstate 70 between Wheeling, West Virginia, and Columbus.

Hanna Coal's "Gem of Egypt," one of the company's two 100-foot-high, 10,000-horsepower electric shovels, with 200-ton buckets the girth of two bulldozers, is digging day and night almost into the backyards of the tiny I-70 town of Hendrysburg in Belmont County, in plain and spectacular view of passing motorists.

In one 24-hour shift, the "Gem"—the name stands for "Giant Earth Mover"—consumes more electricity, generated by coal, than any city in Belmont County. The Egypt Valley strip mine produces nearly 5 million tons of coal a year, most of it shipped in 100-car trains that shuttle back and forth to electric power companies in the Middle West. The mine has nearly obliterated the township of Kirkwood.

. . . Scores of aggrieved persons here have lost well water, have suffered sleepless nights from blasting, or have seen timbered acreage at their property lines turned into 100-foot-deep pits of strip mines.

"They're turning this beautiful place into a desert," says Rep. Wayne Hays, an outspoken Ohio Democrat who lives at Flushing, a Belmont County town isolated on three sides by abandoned strip mine high-walls. . . . "They'll take anything that's black and will burn. . . . It costs them more to really reclaim this land than the land is worth when they're finished. . . ."

The response of Hanna Coal to such criticisms is predictable. It is, after all, a part of Consolidation Coal, whose official attitude was presumably expressed when one of its vice-presidents, James D. Reilly, addressed the American Mining Congress at Pittsburgh in the spring of 1969. According to widely quoted press reports, he declared that conservationists who demand that strip miners do a better job of restoring the lands from which their profits are derived are "stupid idiots, socialists and Commies who don't know what they're talking about. I think it is our bounden duty to knock them down and subject them to the ridicule they deserve." Ralph Hatch, president of Hanna Coal, contented himself with describing the objections of Mr. Hays and people who share them as "emotional" or "sentimental." And he was echoed by Ford Sampson, head of the Ohio Power Association: "What are we going to do? Are we going to cut off the electric power because some guy has a sentimental feeling about an acre of coal?"

Compared with its chief rival, however, Consol is a relative new-comer to strip mining. In two counties of Missouri, thirty years of the practice by Peabody Coal have left an area of flat land covering two hundred square miles an unreclaimed ecological ruin. More recently, Peabody's depredations have spread to the Southwest—where, more frenetically than in any other part of the United States, the pursuit of "growth" has been made synonymous with progress. Since that growth could not have been achieved without water to "make the desert bloom," a nation elsewhere burdened with overproduction has labored for three quarters of a century to add further to the surpluses of wheat, corn, and cotton already in storage. By the same prodigious effort, industrialization underwritten by a government without heed to every natural warning has led to the building in the deserts of Arizona and Nevada of cities that must be supplied with water in their turn.

The marvels of hydrological engineering have indeed brought water to the West. As a result, cotton is being grown in Arizona —and the sufferers from asthma and other respiratory diseases who chose to settle in Phoenix for the benefit of its clear, dry air are feeling the effects. There is smog even in Tucson. And behind the huge dams, the silt is gathering—just as it gathered in Old World reservoirs—while the water turns brackish as its minerals accumulate. There is as yet no persuasive evidence that engineers of the twenty-first century will have discovered any solution to this age-old problem. They can only accelerate the ever more costly search for new sources of water to divert, impound, ditch, and finally pollute.

Nothing in the history of a region filled with ever more grandiose absurdities can surpass the absurdity of the Central Arizona Project. After the outrage of conservationists had spearheaded a campaign to prevent the U.S. Bureau of Reclamation from building a dam in the Grand Canyon, the Bureau was directed by Congress to pump water from the Colorado River to Phoenix and Tucson. To supply the power for the enormous flow of electricity required by these developing cities—not to mention Los Angeles itself—a consortium of twenty-three power companies agreed to build a string of six vast power plants, each one of them to be fired with coal. According to *The New York Times* for May 15, 1971, their generating capacity by 1985 will be thirty-six million kilowatts, or three times the amount generated by the Tennessee Valley Authority.

As of May 1971, two of the plants had already been built—with so little fanfare that nothing in the way of protests or public hearings preceded them. On May 11, five Navajo Indians brought suit against the federal government in an effort to close down the Four Corners Plant at Farmington, New Mexico, because it was polluting the air. On May 14, a group of Hopi Indians brought a suit of their own, calling on the court to declare unlawful the leasing of strip-mine rights in 1968 to the Peabody Coal Company on approximately one hundred square miles of Black Mesa, a region they described as having "special significance in Hopi religion and culture. Carving up Black Mesa by the process known as strip mining," the Hopis said, "is a desecration, a sacrilege, contrary to the instructions of the Great Spirit and to the essential relationship to the land that is embodied in Hopi culture."

Among the Navajos, the reaction was no less bitter. Although a contract had been signed between Navajo elders and representatives of the Peabody Coal Company, a tribal councilman has since said, "The Council has never had good discussion on it. We were asked in effect to say yes or no." An old Navajo mourned, "See that hill? My father and grandfather said that is a holy place. Now, what will happen to that holy place?" And another told of how, like the hill people of Kentucky, he had rushed out and stopped the bulldozers at his doorstep. But the invasion had already begun, the strip mining proceeds, and the plants are being built.[4]

[4] In the controversy over this project, statistics are almost endless. For example, a coal slurry preparation plant at Kaventa, Arizona, was reported to have cost $3.9 million to build. The manager appeared pleased with himself because forty or fifty Indians had helped with the construction, and "about twenty" were being kept on to help run it. At Black Mesa, Gladwin Hill of *The New York Times*, who found all to be well—including Peabody's reclamation plans—reported: "Geologists estimate that there is enough coal there to provide 13 million tons a year for at least 35 years. . . . The coal—low-sulphur anthracite—is ground into powder, mixed with water and sluiced through a 275-mile pipeline to the new Mohave generating plant," which as of January 1971 was turning out "enough electricity for 750,000 people, and in a year or so will be producing twice as much, burning 10 tons of coal a minute, 5 million tons a year. . . . In 1974 a similar plant, half again as big, is scheduled to start operation at Page, Arizona, on the

And what of the day when all six of the projected plants are completed and are burning each day the all-but-unimaginable total of two thousand railroad carloads of strip-mined coal? With the thousands of tons of sulfur and nitrogen oxides that will poison the once clear air, there will be weather inversions to hold and concentrate the pollutants. The water of the Colorado will be heated and consumed in such stupendous quantities that its level of salinity can be expected to rise steadily. Just what the cumulative effect on land, air, and water will be, no one can predict with any exactness—but it is enough to guess that all living things will suffer.

As for the effect on the land from which the coal is mined, that can already be seen at Black Mesa and at Dot Klish Canyon, where the techniques perfected in Appalachia are now being applied with ruthless efficiency. At Black Mesa, the road leading to the strip mines slashes twice across the canyon, traversing natural drains on culvertless fills that guarantee washouts and flooding on a large scale. Where the road ends, amid clouds of dust raised by the giant trucks, bulldozers, high lifts, shovels, and pneumatic drills, and a din equal to that of an artillery barrage, the land—sixty-four thousand acres of it—is being systematically dismembered. Out of it comes the coal that will light the casinos of Las Vegas and the smog-laden freeway of Los Angeles. Out of the aquifers of the surrounding tableland, pumps will suck up water at the rate of two thousand gallons a minute. No one knows what this lowering of the water table may do to the Indians whose

upper reach of the Colorado, 80 miles away. . . . It will get 8 million tons a year of Black Mesa coal, delivered by railroad." The plant at Page will occupy 1,021 acres, plus 765 more for storing fly ash. The stacks will tower to a height of 800 feet, and will disperse into the atmosphere the smoke, soot, dust, and gases from 23,000 tons of coal each day. Forty thousand acre-feet of water will be consumed annually as they flow through the cooling towers at a rate of 270,000 gallons per minute. Its cost will be $328 million, plus another $178 million for the transmission lines to carry away its output.

life depends upon it; but the Indians themselves already fear the worst.

What will become of the Navajos and the Hopis who for so many generations have planted their gardens along the tiny creeks, herding their flocks of goats, sheep, and cattle, holding tenaciously to their villages and their ancient culture? Who has given thought to them? Will they, like the fleeing hill people of Appalachia, end their days in the slums, the jails, and the jail-like housing projects of Los Angeles?

The quiet people of Dot Klish Canyon and Black Mesa were helpless to ward off this impending threat to their ancient way of life. The odds were too great. They were poor and unorganized. Now, those who speak for them say they fear "for the extinction of Hopi life."

And what of the rest of America? What is to become of it?

For a ghastly clue, look again at what is happening in the state of Iowa, underneath whose chocolate-colored, incomparably fertile soil with its square, two-story, white-painted farmhouses lie some twenty-four billion tons of coal. Although by the end of 1964, eleven thousand acres had been strip-mined for that coal, Iowa still has no reclamation law. There is no requirement that the shattered cap rock from above the coal be buried in the pits. The last thing to come from the trenches before the coal is lifted out, that rock is piled atop the heaps of soil that once lay over it. When the operation is completed, gray pools of stagnant water reflect the sky overhead and the formless heaps of soil and rock that tower beside them. Wind and rain carve these heaps gradually into gentler mounds, and the vegetation, returning as a rough garment of weeds and sycamores, struggles to redeem the harsh, unnatural terrain. As the prospects for corn and hogs decline, and the boom in coal and electric power continues, the outlook even for this breadbasket in the heartland of America is frightening.

For several years Iowa's numerous and well-established farm organizations have tried to lobby a reclamation law through the state legislature; but at every turn they have been stymied by a still fledgling coal industry. In Des Moines, coal spokesmen argue that reclamation is a national problem, calling for uniform federal regulations. In Washington, the same lobbyists tell Congressmen that stripping is uniquely a state problem. And so nothing is done at either level—as is in no way surprising to one who agrees with Mark Twain that the main difference between fleas and legislators is that fleas are more educable. Which may in fact be unfair to the fleas.

CHAPTER X

In February 1971, President Nixon said in a message to Congress that he was proposing a bill to regulate strip mining by imposing federal standards for the states. No one was either greatly cheered or unduly alarmed by the announcement. The mining interests and their allies were too well heeled, too thoroughly entrenched to fear a challenge from Congress. A few of its members—notably former Senator Frank Lausche of Ohio, and more recently Senator Gaylord Nelson of Wisconsin, along with Ken Hechler in the House of Representatives—have indeed devoted both thought and effort to the problems raised by the spread of strip mining. But to date this industrial Cosa Nostra has had no federal agencies breathing down its neck.

If Congress as a body were not so lacking in imagination and so difficult to educate, it would long ago have enacted a tough, no-nonsense, three-pronged federal reclamation law. Such a law would have asserted once and for all that the American people are determined to use the land in such a way that it will not be ruined for tomorrow. It would, first of all, permit surface mining only in areas where the degree of slope, the rate of precipitation, type of natural vegetation, and conditions of drainage combined would allow the prompt and effective restoration of the surface to its original character and use; and where stripping is deemed permissible, all the costs of that restoration would be borne by the industry and passed on to consumers as part of the price for steel and electricity. Second, in areas where such restoration cannot be achieved—as it clearly cannot in the hills of Appalachia —surface mining would simply not occur. Third, a severance tax would be levied on all strip-mined minerals, to be paid into a federal trust fund to be used in financing reclamation—insofar as reclamation is possible—of those ravaged lands that are now a reproach to the nation.

In England, Germany, and Czechoslovakia, total reclamation of mined areas is a matter of course; but a reasonable discretion is also exercised in deciding which areas are to be mined. Where circumstances permit stripping to be followed by restoration, the strata are mechanically separated as the earth is peeled away. First the topsoil is scraped back and saved. Next comes the subsoil, which is heaped separately. Next come the rock and slate. Once the underlying coal has been removed, the rock and slate are shoved into the bottom of the pit. The subsoil follows and is compacted with heavy rollers. Then the original topsoil is spread in place and treated with limestone and fertilizers. Seeds are sown and trees are planted. Within five years the scars are healed. Such an outcome is not possible, obviously, on steep, rain-lashed, timbered slopes, or on the sheer sides of a region such as Black Mesa. It could be practiced with ease, on the other hand, in the fields of Iowa, the lignite prairies of the Dakotas, and the ore-bearing regions of Minnesota and Texas. Unfortunately, the process costs huge sums of money. In Britain, the National Coal Board has found the cost to be from a dollar to $1.15 per ton mined—and whereas the British assume that cost, American mining companies are reluctant to spend as much as ten cents a ton, though they have been known to spend lavishly when it comes to opposing reclamation. (A campaign in West Virginia by the Surface Mining Association was reported to have spent $100,000 on advertising its point of view.) As a consequence, mines in Britain and Germany close and U.S. exports soar.

Perhaps the years ahead of us will produce what we most need: advocates for those yet unborn. The present has many voices clamoring on their own behalf: big and little business, farmers, workers, professional groups, the black, red, and Chicano minorities—even welfare recipients—are becoming more or less well organized, and all are demanding more for themselves. Few and muted are those who speak for the millions waiting to be born, to urge that something of the earth's goods be preserved in trust for them. Even conservation groups, overwhelmed by scores of environmental challenges, have somehow been lacking in either the energy or the funds to mount a full-scale effort in defense of the nation's ravaged landscape. On March 2, 1971, however, a suit was entered in a U.S. District Court by three such organizations —the Natural Resources Defense Council, Inc., the Environmental Defense Fund, and the Sierra Club, seeking to void strip-mining contracts entered into by the Tennessee Valley Authority with various suppliers and valued at $111 million, and asking further for "a cease to strip mining and purchasing of strip-mined coal" by the agency.

The far-reaching significance of this action is clear from an editorial published in *The New York Times* on December 22, 1970, some months before the suit was filed. Entitled "The Great Soil Swindle," it pointed out that "in the 1930's the Federal Government undertook numerous and costly soil conservation programs when windstorms turned the prairies into a dust bowl. Yet the Government today stands by, silently, impotently, as coal operators lay waste the land and scatter topsoil as recklessly as the dust storms ever did. Why the contrast? The answer can only be that nobody made money out of the dust storms, but the Consolidation Coal Company, the TVA and other private and public entrepreneurs are profiting from the rape of the land."

A few days afterward, the *Times* carried in reply the latest bland pronouncement by Aubrey Wagner, chairman of the board of TVA, welcoming the "concern expressed" but rejecting "the easy answer," namely the outlawing of strip mining, advocated by the *Times*. Why? The answer may, perhaps, be found in a statement from the agency's annual report—that the "TVA brings critically needed broad perspective to today's most crucial national challenge: the use of technology to protect the environment even as it enhances the quality of man's existence."

In such burbling phrases the litany goes on, exalting almost to the condition of deity what is in fact a national disease: the use of technology as a thing somehow unquestionably good, regardless of the consequences. How else are we to account for a disruption so callous that even the dead are no longer permitted to lie in peace? In Knott County, Kentucky, Mrs. Bige Ritchie saw the coffin of her infant son flung up by a bulldozer. In Arizona, a Navajo woman told of seeing a gravesite disturbed when the strippers came to Black Mesa. And in Belmont County, Ohio, a local historian, Mrs. Donald Stobbs, told Ben Franklin that an unmarked Quaker graveyard containing the last earthly remains of William Milhous Sr. and Jr., the great-great-great- and great-great-grandfathers of Richard Nixon, had been leased for stripping. "It seems like no one cares," she said.

In Vietnam, of course, not caring has become merely a part of the routine. "Land clearing" to deny the enemy a place to hide goes on daily, using Rome Plows—giant army bulldozers that obliterate dikes, rice fields, houses, and enemy bunkers without discrimination. "We leave the old graves, because they're sacred to the people who used to live here," a Rome Plow platoon leader explained to a reporter. "But we dig up the new graves, because usually they're just enemy caches. How do I decide about houses? Well, if it don't have anybody in it we knock them down."

And so the use of technology goes mindlessly on and on. The same editorial page that carried Chairman Wagner's letter rejecting "the easy answer" also carried a troubled comment on the report that the use of defoliants had reduced much of the mangrove forest of South Vietnam to "a man-made wasteland that appears incapable of producing new vegetation."

It is to this that the worship of technology has brought us and our own land as well. As an Ohio Congressman, John Seiberling, put it, "The Romans created a desert and called it peace. We create a desert and call it progress."

And that desert is the only land Americans will ever have.